The QUICK & EASY
SPICED NICE
COOKBOOK

60 Exciting Meals
That Deliver on Flavor—
in 30 Minutes or Less

Farrah Jalanbo

Creator of Spiced.Nice

PAGE STREET
PUBLISHING CO.

PAGE STREET
PUBLISHING CO.

First published in 2022 by

Page Street Publishing Co.

27 Congress Street, Suite 1511

Salem, MA 01970

www.pagestreetpublishing.com

Distributed by Macmillan, sales in Canada by The Canadian Manda Group.

26   25   24   23   22   2   3   4   5

ISBN-13: 978-1-64567-490-0

ISBN-10: 1-64567-490-8

Library of Congress Control Number: 2021938435

Cover and book design by Molly Kate Young for Page Street Publishing Co.

Photography by Farrah Jalanbo

Printed and bound in the United States

DEDICATION

This book is dedicated to my mother, Abir, my father, Ziad, and my husband, Tarek.

Mama and Baba: Thank you for giving me a lovely childhood that fostered this passion for cooking. The kindness, love and patience with which you treated me gave way to my creativity and has taught me how to put my heart and soul into each and every recipe. Everything I am is because of you.

Tarek: This book is possible because of your support. You encouraged me to start my food blog while on our honeymoon, so thank you for believing in me more than I believed in myself at the time. You've held my hand through every step of the way, and I could not have done it without you.

Contents

INTRODUCTION

Cooking is my love language. It's my favorite way to tell someone I appreciate them, I'm sorry or that I love them. Many of my earliest childhood memories revolve around cooking. Whether it be making Sunday morning breakfast with my dad, closely observing my mom's impressive kitchen skills or whipping up something completely random whenever I had the kitchen to myself, cooking was a clear passion from age seven. One of the earliest dishes I can remember making is maacarona bil laban, which is a version of my Syrian Garlic Yogurt Pasta (page 102). At each sleepover with my friends, I would try to involve cooking in some way. I often suggested we all cook something for fun, and it was a tradition for me to make them ful, a Middle Eastern fava bean breakfast dish.

I could never seem to peel myself away from the kitchen. I always had the urge to create new meals and satisfy any craving I had by making the food myself. I would combine all sorts of flavors and ingredients until something delicious was made of it. As a young child, there was one week when I was obsessed with perfecting a homemade marinara sauce. I would sit in class, eager to get home so I could try again. First, I tried to make it with tomato paste, simple spices, water, etc. In the next attempt, I used tomato sauce, a few more spices and some sautéed garlic. After a few trials, I ended up using fresh tomatoes and garlic, which I blistered in olive oil with fresh herbs and spices and simmered with liquid until the sauce was pure perfection. Being a high-energy child, I unfortunately tended to leave an absolute mess in the kitchen, and my poor mother would have to go in and do some major damage control. According to her, it was "a hurricane" every time I stepped foot into the kitchen. I used to climb onto the countertops and stand on them so I could reach the spice cabinets, knocking over absolutely anything in my way. I'd use a small stepping stool to reach the stovetop only to splatter and fling the food and sauces all over.

My favorite part about cooking has always been feeding others. There's nothing like the feeling of seeing your loved ones gather at a table, smiling, chatting and enjoying the food you've cooked for them. I truly believe the way to someone's heart is through their stomach. Taking the time and energy to please someone by making them a good meal is something they'll cherish forever. When I was younger, I was home alone with my dad one evening. He's always been my best friend, so I figured we'd have some fun. I told him to get ready for a five-course meal that I was going to cook for him, plate nicely and serve him. Keep in mind: My mom was not home to tell me I couldn't make a mess, so I really had to take advantage. Of course, he was all in for this activity. I served him fattoush salad, spaghetti, tacos, among other things, and each plate was carefully decorated and then served. I'll never forget how good it felt watching my dad's face light up each time I'd bring out the new dish and he'd take the first bite. More than fifteen years later, my dad still frequently tells this story with the proudest smile on his face to anyone who will listen.

Growing up in a Syrian American household in California with close family friends of varying ethnic backgrounds has had a strong influence on the types of food I cook. At home, we grew up eating a lot of Middle Eastern, Mexican and South Asian food. In this book, you'll find many fusion recipes, classics with my Spiced Nice twist to them and extremely flavorful recipes that are inspired by several different cuisines. The priority of this book is to provide you with quick, yet mouth-watering recipes for a busy weeknight when you could use a comforting home-cooked meal. I've included a chapter on healthy recipes because one of the most common questions I get is, "How can I eat healthy without getting bored of the same plain chicken and salad?" Well, you *don't* have to sacrifice variety or flavor when it comes to wanting something quick and/or healthy. You'll also get your fix of fun "weekend" type meals, along with Middle Eastern and fusion foods, pastas and recipes using the trendy Instant Pot and air fryer gadgets. Most importantly, you'll find recipes that are carefully crafted and made with love in order to spread the joy of food and cooking from my home into yours.

Farrah Jalanbo

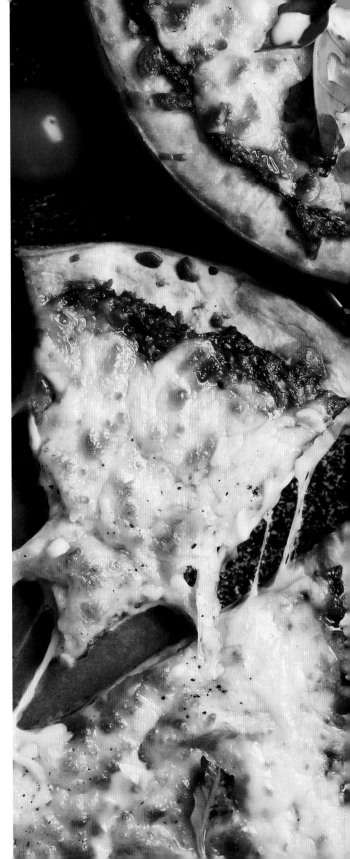

CHAPTER 1:
WHY WAIT *for the* WEEKEND?

This chapter is for all my party people. By party, I mean food hopping and trying hole-in-the-wall spots on the weekends. From tacos to juicy cheeseburgers, noodles, crispy fried chicken, loaded nachos and much more, this chapter summarizes what the adventures of a foodie's successful weekend might look like. Fun recipes, trendy foods and incredible flavors are brought on heavy here. The food we eat holds so much power, and the recipes in this chapter will make you feel good through excitement and a satisfied belly. If you are what you eat, I truly wouldn't mind being a fiery chicken cutlet (page 11). Yum!

CRISPY CHICKEN CUTLETS WITH A FIERY GARLIC SAUCE

Why go out for a bite to eat when these fast-and-easy chicken cutlets check all the boxes? Juicy, extremely crispy, slightly sweet, slightly spicy and garlicky: Need I say more? Pair it with some sticky white rice and a cold drink, and then put your feet up and relax. You deserve this meal!

Yield: 2 servings

For the Fiery Garlic Sauce

¼ cup (60 g) sambal chili paste

1 tsp crushed garlic

1½ tbsp (23 ml) honey

¼ tsp minced ginger

For the Breading

½ cup (63 g) all-purpose flour

1 tsp cayenne, divided

2 tsp (5 g) garlic powder, divided

¾ tsp black pepper, divided

1 tsp salt, divided

2 eggs

1 tsp sambal chili paste (or substitute with 2 tsp [10 ml] hot sauce)

1 cup (56 g) plain panko bread crumbs

1 tbsp (7 g) paprika

For the Chicken

1 lb (454 g) chicken breast, sliced into ½" (1.3-cm)-thick fillets*

Vegetable oil, for frying

1 thinly sliced scallion, for garnishing

* For a major time-saver, I purchase thinly sliced chicken breast fillets at the market. You can also ask the butcher to fillet the chicken for you!

1. To make the fiery garlic sauce, in a small bowl, whisk together the sambal chili paste, crushed garlic, honey and ginger. Set aside.

2. To prepare the breading, in a large bowl, whisk together the flour, ¼ teaspoon of the cayenne, 1½ teaspoons (4 g) of the garlic powder, ¼ teaspoon of the pepper and ¼ teaspoon of the salt. In a small bowl, whisk together the eggs and the sambal chili paste. On a plate, mix together the panko, paprika and the remaining cayenne, garlic powder, pepper and salt.

3. To prepare the chicken, one by one, evenly coat each fillet in the flour mixture. Shake off any excess flour, and then dredge the fillet in the wet mixture until fully coated. Drip any excess mixture off, and then coat in the bread crumb mixture. Be sure every crack and crevice is coated.

4. In a shallow frying pan, heat 1½ inches (4 cm) of the oil until the temperature reaches 350°F (180°C). Fry the cutlets for 2 minutes on each side, or until golden. Remove the chicken and place it on a cooling rack so that the excess oil drips off and the chicken stays crispy. Serve the crispy cutlets with the fiery garlic sauce and top with sliced scallions.

THE BEST CHEESY SMASH BURGERS

Smash burgers are my weakness and these ones are the BEST . . . trust me on this one! Juicy, flavorful, and they have those perfect smash burger crispy edges. The meat is seasoned well with smoky and peppery flavors and is melt-in-your-mouth amazing. Serve these with some crispy fries or your favorite side. You can also enjoy them in a lettuce wrap for a delicious low-carb option!

Yield: 4 servings

For the Sauce
¼ cup + 1 tbsp (75 ml) mayonnaise

2 tbsp (30 ml) ketchup

1½ tbsp (23 ml) sweet relish

1 tsp sugar

½ tbsp (8 ml) vinegar

For the Burgers
1 lb (454 g) 80% lean ground beef

2 tsp (10 ml) Worcestershire sauce

1 tsp salt

½ tsp black pepper

¾ tsp garlic powder

½ tsp liquid smoke (optional)

Sliced cheese of choice (I use American)

For the Buns and Serving
½ tbsp (7 g) butter

4 brioche buns

Onions

Sliced pickles (optional)

1. To make the sauce, in a small bowl, mix together the mayonnaise, ketchup, sweet relish, sugar and vinegar. Set aside.

2. To make the burgers, in a large bowl, add the beef, Worcestershire sauce, salt, pepper, garlic powder and liquid smoke (if using) and mix together until just combined. Be sure not to overmix as that tends to make your patties tougher. Separate the meat into four equal balls.

3. Place a griddle or skillet over medium-high heat, and once very hot, add the meat balls. Use a heavy object like a cast-iron skillet to smash them down until spread very thin. You may have to cook in batches depending on how large your skillet is. Cook for about 2 minutes, or until each patty has that signature smash-burger crisp, and then flip and let the other side cook through. Immediately add the sliced cheese on top after flipping the patties.

4. As the burgers are cooking, prepare the buns by placing the butter in a separate skillet or griddle. Once hot, add the buns to toast the insides.

5. Spread the burger sauce onto the bottom bun, and then top with the patty, onions and pickles, if using. Complete with the top bun then dig in!

GARLIC CILANTRO STEAK TACOS

This tender, juicy steak is loaded up with cilantro and garlicky goodness. Paired with my special creamy green sauce, these tacos are just unforgettable. Late-night taco trucks in the city have nothing on a quiet weeknight at home, munching down on these. Every component in these tacos is packed with flavor, and it's a delightful shock to your taste buds when you take that first bite. Enjoy this on your own or with friends and family for a meal they'll absolutely love you for making.

Yield: 4 servings

For the Steak and Marinade

2 lb (907 g) flap meat or boneless steak of choice

1 bunch cilantro

¼ onion

3 tbsp (45 ml) lime juice

4 cloves garlic

1½ tsp (9 g) salt

¾ tsp black pepper

1 tsp cumin

5 tbsp (75 ml) olive oil, divided

½ jalapeño (optional)

For the Creamy Green Sauce

1 bunch cilantro

¼ cup (60 ml) lime juice

5 cloves garlic

½ jalapeño

½ cup (120 ml) sour cream

½ cup (116 g) cream cheese

1 tsp salt

For Assembling and Serving

Mini corn or flour street taco tortillas, heated

1 sliced avocado

Diced red onions

Chopped cilantro

Cotija cheese (optional)

Lime wedges

1. To prepare the steak and marinade, cut the steak into taco-size bits (½-inch [1.3-cm] pieces). Prepare the marinade by combining the cilantro, onion, lime juice, garlic, salt, pepper, cumin, 3 tablespoons (45 ml) of the olive oil and jalapeño (if using) in a blender. Blend until a smooth, dark green sauce has formed. Pour the marinade over the cut steak and set it aside to marinate.

2. For the creamy green sauce, combine the cilantro, lime juice, garlic, jalapeño, sour cream, cream cheese and salt in a blender. Blend until a creamy, light green sauce has formed.

3. Heat a skillet over high heat and add the remaining oil until it's very hot. Using tongs, drip off any excess marinade and place the steak on the hot skillet. Cook for 5 minutes, or until cooked to your liking.

4. To assemble the tacos, spoon the hot, juicy steak onto the mini tortillas. Layer on the sliced avocado, onions, a generous drizzle of the creamy green sauce, a sprinkle of chopped cilantro and crumbled Cotija cheese (if using). Serve with lime wedges.

SPICY BEEF UDON SOUP

A big, comforting bowl of this soup is exactly what I need every time the temperature dips below 80°F in California. I know that's still hot, but that's my point. This. Soup. Is. Always. Delicious. The aromatic flavors will tickle your taste buds and have you licking your bowl clean. Feel free to make it your own by swapping beef for chicken, or make it completely vegan by adding tofu and mushrooms with a vegetable broth.

Yield: 3 servings

1 lb (454 g) ribeye steak

3½ tsp (18 ml) soy sauce, divided

1 tbsp (15 ml) vegetable oil, plus more as needed

5 cloves garlic

1" (2.5-cm) piece ginger, peeled

3 dried red chiles

1 cinnamon stick

2 star anise

½ tsp whole coriander

½ tsp black peppercorns

2 bay leaves

¼ onion

4 cups (960 ml) low-sodium beef broth

1 cup (240 ml) vegetable broth

1 quarter-size piece yellow rock sugar or 1¼ tsp (6 g) granulated sugar

1 tsp chili bean sauce

¾ tsp fish sauce

¼ tsp Chinese five-spice powder

9 oz (255 g) udon noodles

Salt, to taste

Optional Toppings

Bean sprouts

Lime wedges

Chopped cilantro

Sliced scallions

Sliced jalapeños

Sliced onions

1. Thinly slice the ribeye steak into ½-inch (1.3-cm) strips. Toss with 1½ teaspoons (8 ml) of the soy sauce and set aside. In a wok or deep pan, heat the vegetable oil over high heat. Once hot, add the steak and quickly sear until browned on all sides, but not yet fully cooked internally. Remove the steak and set aside.

2. Lower the heat to medium-high, and if needed, add a little more oil to the wok or pan, and then toss in the garlic and ginger. Quickly sauté until fragrant, and then add the red chiles, cinnamon stick, star anise, coriander, black peppercorns, bay leaves and onion. Toast all this together for 2 minutes, or until the spices are fragrant and the garlic, ginger and onion have some color on them.

3. Pour in the beef and vegetable broths, and add the rock sugar, remaining soy sauce, chili bean sauce, fish sauce and Chinese five-spice. Let this come to a boil, and then lower the heat to medium-low and simmer for 10 minutes. Strain the broth through a fine-mesh strainer into a heatproof bowl. Return the clear broth to the wok or pan and add the steak and the udon noodles. Boil over medium-high heat for 5 minutes, or until the steak and noodles are cooked through. Taste the broth and add salt if needed. Serve with any or all of the optional toppings.

ELOTES QUESADILLAS

After taking one bite of this quesadilla, I yelled as loudly as I could for my husband to come downstairs and try it immediately. It was that good. It truly wowed me, and I cannot wait for you to try it! The elotes flavors we all love are paired with a food no one can really fault: quesadillas. Crispy, cheesy, creamy, smoky . . . just describing it has me itching to make some more.

Yield: 3 servings

2 tbsp (30 ml) olive oil, divided

1 cup (154 g) corn

½ tsp paprika

¾ tsp smoked paprika

½ tsp chili powder

½ tsp garlic powder

½ tsp black pepper

¼ tsp salt, plus more to taste

1½ tbsp (23 ml) mayonnaise

¼ cup (60 ml) crema Mexicana

Juice of ½ lime

1 tbsp (15 ml) adobo sauce

2 cups (224 g) shredded mozzarella

1½ tbsp (9 g) Cotija cheese, divided

1 tbsp (2 g) finely chopped cilantro

3 flour tortillas

1. In a wide skillet, heat 1 tablespoon (15 ml) of the olive oil over high heat. Once hot, add the corn and season it with the paprika, smoked paprika, chili powder, garlic powder, pepper and ¼ teaspoon of salt. Stir and then leave the corn to char for 2 minutes before stirring again. Turn off the heat and mix in the mayonnaise, and then set the corn aside in a bowl to cool.

2. For our sauce, combine the crema Mexicana, lime juice, adobo sauce and a pinch of salt to taste in a blender. Blend until smooth.

3. Mix the corn in a large bowl with the mozzarella cheese, 1 tablespoon (6 g) of the Cotija cheese and the finely chopped cilantro. In the skillet, heat the remaining olive oil over medium-high heat. Add a flour tortilla (make one quesadilla at a time) and quickly heat it on one side for 1 minute, and then flip it over. As the other side heats up, sprinkle an even layer of the corn and cheese mixture onto the top. Don't get too close to the edges so the cheese doesn't melt out and burn.

4. Lower the heat to medium and allow the bottom side of the tortilla to crisp up as the cheese melts. Take a peek and once the bottom of the tortilla is starting to look golden, cover the pan with a lid to speed up the cheese melting. Cook for 2 minutes, or until the cheese is fully melted. Use a spatula to fold the tortilla over in half. Remove and let it rest for 1 minute before slicing into the quesadilla.

5. Repeat until all the quesadillas are cooked. Serve hot and top with a drizzle of the adobo lime sauce and a sprinkle of the remaining Cotija cheese.

Note: Refrigerate the corn and cheese mixture as well as the adobo lime sauce in separate containers and have the ingredients ready for an even quicker meal throughout the week!

HERBED CHICKEN GYROS

These chicken gyros (yiros) take me back to Greece. They're zesty, herby and filled with my favorite Mediterranean flavors. Traditionally, the meat is cooked on a spit and carved off into thin pieces. For this recipe, we did a much quicker version that packs the same amount of flavor in a shorter time. The chicken is seasoned with garlic and herb flavors and sits perfectly in a fluffy Greek pita.

Yield: 3 servings

¾ cup (180 ml) Greek yogurt

2 tbsp + 2 tsp (40 ml) olive oil, divided

1 tbsp (15 ml) lemon juice

1 tsp crushed garlic

¼ tsp cumin

½ tsp black pepper

½ tsp onion powder

½ tsp paprika

⅛ tsp cayenne

1 tsp dried oregano

1 tsp dried thyme

1 tsp salt, or to taste

1 lb (454 g) thinly sliced boneless, skinless chicken thighs or breast (chicken fillets)

For Serving

Greek pitas

Tzatziki

Sliced tomato

Thinly sliced red onion

Shredded iceberg lettuce (optional)

Feta cheese (optional)

1. In a large bowl, add the Greek yogurt, 2 teaspoons (10 ml) of the olive oil, lemon juice, crushed garlic, cumin, pepper, onion powder, paprika, cayenne, oregano, thyme and salt. Mix well. Add the chicken and score it by puncturing a knife through the pieces a few times. (This ensures the marinade flavors the chicken all the way through.) Set aside to marinate while you prepare the remaining ingredients. If you have the time, I HIGHLY recommend marinating the night before so the yogurt has ample time to work its magic and tenderize the chicken.

2. Heat the remaining olive oil in a skillet over medium-high heat. Once the oil is hot, drip off the excess marinade from the chicken fillets and place them into the skillet. Be sure not to overcrowd the skillet. Cook on each side for 2 to 3 minutes, depending on the thickness of your fillets, or until the juices have dried and the chicken is cooked through.

3. Slice the chicken fillets into thin strips. Assemble each sandwich with a heated Greek pita, a spread of tzatziki, tomato, onion, chicken and optional lettuce and/or feta.

CHILI LIME SHRIMP TACOS WITH CILANTRO CREMA

These shrimp tacos are the quickest taco recipe in the book, taking just under 15 minutes to make! They're quick, but absolutely delicious, and don't be fooled by the short cook time because the flavors in these are well and alive. Chili lime juicy shrimp paired with a creamy, garlicky cilantro crema . . . it doesn't get any better (or quicker!) than this.

Yield: 2 servings

For the Cilantro Crema

½ bunch cilantro, plus more for serving

2 tbsp (30 ml) lime juice

2 cloves garlic

⅓ cup (80 ml) crema Mexicana

½ tsp black pepper

½ tsp salt

For the Shrimp

1½ tbsp (23 ml) olive oil

1 lb (454 g) shrimp, peeled and deveined, tails off

½ tsp chili powder

½ tsp cumin

½ tsp black pepper

½ tsp smoked paprika

½ tsp paprika

1 tsp garlic powder

¾ tsp onion powder

1 tbsp (15 ml) lime juice

Salt, to taste

For Serving

Mini corn or flour street taco tortillas, heated

Pico de gallo

Sliced avocados

Lime wedges

1. To make the crema, add the cilantro, lime juice, garlic, crema Mexicana, pepper and salt to a blender. Blend until a light green, creamy sauce forms. Set aside.

2. To make the shrimp, heat the olive oil in a skillet over medium-high heat. Add the shrimp and season with the chili powder, cumin, pepper, smoked paprika, paprika, garlic powder, onion powder, lime juice and salt. Toss the shrimp and cook until the shrimp is pink, about 3 minutes.

3. Assemble the tacos by adding a generous spoonful of shrimp to the tortillas, followed by the pico de gallo, sliced avocado and the cilantro crema.

SESAME GINGER BEEF BULGOGI

I've always loved beef bulgogi. The slightly sweet and nutty flavors always satisfy my taste buds and this version is no exception. The tender, juicy bulgogi steak is flavored perfectly with the sesame, pear, ginger and garlic marinade. Enjoy this recipe with some steamed rice and vegetables or with some garlic noodles.

Yield: 2 servings

2 tbsp (30 g) finely diced onion

1 Asian pear, peeled and deseeded

6 cloves garlic

½" (1.3-cm) piece ginger

3 tbsp (45 ml) soy sauce

1 tbsp (15 ml) sesame oil

¼ tsp white pepper

1¼ tsp (4 g) brown sugar

1 lb (454 g) boneless steak, thinly sliced (I use ribeye but flank steak is a popular choice as well)

1½ tbsp (23 ml) vegetable oil

Toasted sesame seeds, for garnishing

Sliced scallions, for garnishing

1. Add the onion, pear, garlic, ginger, soy sauce, sesame oil, white pepper and brown sugar to a blender. Blend until a smooth sauce has formed. Combine with the steak in a large bowl and mix evenly. Cover and marinate for at least 15 minutes, but preferably longer if you have the time.

2. Heat the vegetable oil in a skillet over medium-high heat. Once hot, add the steak and cook on each side for 2 to 3 minutes, or until browned on all sides. Be sure not to overcrowd the pan and cook in batches if necessary. Garnish with the toasted sesame seeds and sliced scallions.

THE ULTIMATE LOADED NACHOS

These nachos will get you through the week. They truly live up to the name—they're layered with a delicious, gooey three-cheese blend and are topped with all the best nacho fixings. A smoky chipotle crema is drizzled all over to finish off this unforgettable treat. Share with some friends or kick back and enjoy it all by yourself!

Yield: 4 servings

For the Chipotle Crema
½ cup (120 ml) crema Mexicana
1 chipotle pepper
¼ tsp salt
½ tsp adobo sauce

For the Nachos
1 (16-oz [454-g]) can refried beans
¼ cup (60 ml) water
1 (6-oz [156-g]) bag tortilla chips
½ cup (57 g) shredded mozzarella cheese
½ cup (57 g) shredded cheddar cheese
½ cup (57 g) shredded Mexican cheese blend
1 avocado
1 tsp lime juice
Salt, to taste
¼ cup (60 ml) sour cream
½ cup (120 ml) salsa
½ cup (80 g) thinly sliced red onions
¼ cup (45 g) sliced olives
¼ cup (29 g) sliced radishes
½ cup (125 g) pickled jalapeños
¼ cup (4 g) chopped cilantro

1. Preheat the oven to 425°F (220°C). Line a sheet tray with parchment paper.

2. To make the chipotle crema, add the crema Mexicana, chipotle pepper, salt and adobo sauce to a blender. Blend until a creamy pink sauce has formed. Set aside.

3. To make the nachos, in a saucepan, add the refried beans and water and stir. Cook over medium heat until heated through.

4. Layer half of the tortilla chips on the sheet tray. Sprinkle on half of the shredded mozzarella, cheddar and Mexican cheese blend. Spoon on half of the refried beans. Repeat and layer on the remaining tortilla chips, mozzarella, cheddar, Mexican cheese blend and refried beans.

5. Bake for 12 minutes, or until the cheese has melted. In a small bowl, mash the avocado and mix with the lime juice and salt. Spoon the mashed avocado on top of the baked nachos and add a dollop of sour cream and salsa in the center. Sprinkle on the red onions, olives, radishes, pickled jalapeños and chopped cilantro. Drizzle on the chipotle crema and dig in!

BARBECUE CHICKEN SLIDERS

Melt-in-your-mouth BBQ chicken sliders . . . it doesn't get any easier and more delicious than this! The chicken is coated in a thick BBQ sauce with complementing spices, melted cheese, a touch of red onions for a slight crunch and soft Hawaiian rolls. The simple garlic butter on top just ties the entire dish together—you'll love it! It's the perfect quick meal on any given night.

Yield: 4 servings

For the Sliders

3 cups (672 g) shredded cooked chicken (see Note)

1¾ cups (420 ml) barbecue sauce of choice, divided

½ tsp garlic powder

½ tsp smoked paprika

¼ tsp onion powder

¼ tsp black pepper

12 Hawaiian sweet rolls

½ cup (57 g) shredded Monterey Jack and cheddar cheese blend

⅓ cup (53 g) diced red onions

For the Garlic Butter

1 stick (½ cup [120 ml]) melted butter

1 tsp garlic powder

Salt, to taste

½ tbsp (2 g) fresh chopped parsley

1. Preheat the oven to 350°F (180°C). Line a 9 x 13–inch (23 x 33–cm) baking dish with aluminum foil.

2. In a large bowl, combine the shredded chicken, 1½ cups (360 ml) of the barbecue sauce, garlic powder, smoked paprika, onion powder and pepper until the chicken is fully coated and sticky.

3. Slice the rolls to separate the top buns from the bottom buns. Place the bottom buns in the baking dish and evenly layer on the chicken mixture, the remaining barbecue sauce, the cheese and the onions. Place on the top buns and cover the dish with foil. Bake for 15 minutes, or until the cheese has completely melted.

4. Meanwhile, prepare the garlic butter by mixing together the melted butter, garlic powder, salt and parsley in a small bowl. Remove the sliders from the oven and brush the garlic butter onto the top buns. Stick the sliders back into the oven, uncovered now, for 5 minutes, or until the top buns are slightly toasted.

Note: I shred up a cooked rotisserie chicken from the market. However, you can also heat 1 teaspoon of oil in a skillet over medium-high heat, and cook two chicken breasts for 8 minutes (4 minutes on each side), or until the internal temperature reaches 165°F (75°C). Season lightly with salt. Once the chicken cools, shred it using two forks.

CHICKEN POMODORI PANINI

This right here is what true love really is. The crunch of the garlic-buttered sourdough bread, with the gooey melted cheese, seasoned chicken, caramelized roasted tomatoes, garlicky pesto mayo and fresh basil and spinach is truly unmatched. Inspired by a panini I had years ago at a bakery, this recipe never fails to wow every guest who tries it.

Yield: 1 serving

For the Chicken
½ chicken breast

4 tsp (20 ml) olive oil, divided

½ tsp black pepper, plus more as needed

¼ tsp garlic powder

¼ tsp salt, plus more as needed

¼ tsp dried oregano

1 Roma tomato, sliced into thin rounds

For the Garlic Butter Bread
1½ tbsp (21 g) salted butter, softened

¼ tsp garlic powder

¼ tsp dried oregano

⅛ tsp black pepper

2 slices sourdough bread

For the Pesto Mayonnaise
2 tbsp (30 ml) mayonnaise

2 tsp (10 ml) pesto

1 clove garlic, crushed

For Serving
2 slices provolone cheese

5 spinach leaves

5 basil leaves

Note: If you have leftover chicken breast from a barbecue, it saves a lot of time to slice it very thinly and use it. In fact, I often make this recipe specifically when I have leftover chicken I want to use up!

1. Set the oven to broil. Line a baking sheet with aluminum foil. To prepare the chicken, working from top to bottom, slice the chicken breast into very thin, ¼-inch (6-mm) slices. You want the slices to resemble thinly shaved chicken after it's cooked. In a bowl, add the chicken, 2 teaspoons (10 ml) of the olive oil, pepper, garlic powder, salt and oregano and mix until the chicken is evenly coated. Cover and set aside.

2. Arrange the sliced tomato rounds onto the baking sheet. Drizzle 1 teaspoon of the olive oil on top of the tomatoes along with a dash of salt and pepper. Broil for 3 minutes, or until softened and slightly roasted. Keep a close eye on these so that they don't burn as every broiler works slightly differently. Once the tomatoes are ready, remove and set aside.

3. Add the remaining olive oil to a skillet and heat it over medium-high heat. Once hot, add the chicken. Since the chicken is so thin, it only needs to be cooked for 1 to 2 minutes per side. Set aside.

4. To make the garlic butter bread, mix the butter, garlic powder, oregano and pepper in a small bowl. Spread the garlic butter on the outer sides of both slices of bread. Place the slices on a hot pan and toast for 2 minutes per side (2 minutes total if using a panini press), or until the bread is a very light gold on both sides. We don't want to fully toast the bread yet since we will be cooking it more later! To make the pesto mayonnaise, mix the mayonnaise, pesto and crushed garlic in a small bowl.

5. To serve, generously spread the pesto mayo on the inside of one sourdough slice. Add a slice of provolone on top. On the other slice of bread, add the second slice of provolone. Now layer on the chicken, tomatoes, spinach and basil. Add the other sourdough slice on top.

6. If using a panini press, cook for 5 minutes, or until the cheese is melted and the bread is golden and crispy. If using a pan, set the heat to medium-high and once the pan gets hot, add the sandwich and press down with a spatula. Cook for about 2 minutes, or until the bread has toasted, and then flip. While pressing down with the spatula, cook for another 2 minutes, or until the bread is golden and the cheese is melted. Remove from the heat and slice in half. Serve immediately.

SPICY POPCORN CHICKEN

Whoever said you can't have fun on weeknights seriously needs a plate of this ultra-crispy, perfectly seasoned popcorn chicken. It's fun, delicious and you can get super-creative with how you eat it. You can serve these with French fries and your favorite dipping sauces, toss in buffalo sauce for some boneless wing action, make a crispy chicken salad or wrap, etc.!

Yield: 4 servings

1 cup (240 ml) buttermilk

1 tbsp (15 ml) hot sauce of choice

1 egg

2 chicken breasts, cut into ¾" (2-cm) popcorn-size pieces

¾ cup (94 g) all-purpose flour

¾ tsp baking powder

¼ cup (32 g) cornstarch

2½ tsp (15 g) salt

1 tsp garlic powder

½ tsp onion powder

½ tsp black pepper

½ tsp smoked paprika

2 tsp (4 g) paprika

¼ tsp cayenne

½ tsp lemon pepper

Oil, for frying

1. In a large bowl, whisk together the buttermilk, hot sauce and egg. Add the chicken and mix until coated. Cover and set aside to marinate for a minimum of 10 minutes, but I recommend marinating for as long as you can. If you have time to do this step the night before, the chicken will be even juicier!

2. In a medium bowl, whisk together the flour, baking powder, cornstarch, salt, garlic powder, onion powder, pepper, smoked paprika, paprika, cayenne and lemon pepper.

3. Drip any excess wet mixture off the chicken pieces, and then fully coat the chicken in the dry mixture. This works best when you only dredge three or four pieces at a time. For extra-crispy chicken, double coat the pieces by dipping them back into the wet mixture once more, and then back into the dry mixture again. This is optional as it will be a thicker coat and take a few more minutes, but I love to do it! Set aside on a tray.

4. Heat up 3 inches (8 cm) of oil in a deep pot until the temperature reaches 350°F (180°C). Test the oil by adding one chicken piece. It should immediately start to bubble and rise to the top as it gradually deepens in color. Add the chicken to the oil and fry for 3 to 4 minutes, or until golden on the outside and cooked through. Be sure not to overcrowd the pot, and you may have to fry the chicken in two batches if your pot is smaller. Once fried, place on a cooling rack to drip off any excess oil so that the chicken stays crispy. Serve with your favorite dipping sauces.

FAN FAVORITE TACO BEEF

This is a Spiced Nice classic and is wildly popular with anyone who makes it! The reviews on my page about this one speak for themselves. This is juicy, flavorful taco beef like you've never had before . . . and it will quickly turn into a favorite in your home. Skip the greasy fast food and opt for this quality, delicious homemade treat!

Yield: 3 servings

1 tbsp (4 g) dried onion flakes

1 tsp cumin

½ tsp cayenne (adjust to preferred spice level)

1 tbsp (7 g) paprika

½ tbsp (3 g) chili powder

1 tsp garlic powder

1 tsp onion powder

½ tsp black pepper

1 tsp dried oregano

½ tsp sugar

Pinch of salt

1 tbsp (15 ml) olive oil

1 lb (454 g) ground beef

2½ tbsp (40 g) tomato paste

⅓ cup (80 ml) low-sodium beef broth

2 tbsp (30 ml) Taco Bell™ Hot Sauce* (optional but recommended)

Taco shells or soft tortillas, heated

Favorite taco fixings, for serving

* Can be found in most grocery stores and online.

1. In a medium bowl, add the dried onion flakes, cumin, cayenne, paprika, chili powder, garlic powder, onion powder, pepper, oregano, sugar and salt.

2. Heat the olive oil in a skillet over medium-high heat, and then add the ground beef. Immediately start to break it down as much as possible. Add in the spice mix and stir. Stir in the tomato paste while continuing to break up the meat. Lower the heat to medium and cook for 7 minutes. Stir occasionally and continue to break down the meat as needed. Pour in the beef broth and Taco Bell Hot Sauce (if using). Let this simmer for 3 to 4 minutes. You should have a saucy ground beef to work with now!

3. Serve the taco beef in hard shells or soft tortillas and top with your favorite taco fixings. Add a side of sour cream and any other taco favorites!

BETTER-THAN-TAKEOUT VEGETABLE LO MEIN

This vegetable lo mein only takes fifteen minutes to make and will satisfy your noodle craving. The noodles are coated with a perfectly thick sauce and are tossed with fresh vegetables to make this your new go-to weeknight dish.

Yield: 4 servings

For the Lo Mein Sauce

3 tbsp (45 ml) oyster sauce

1 tbsp (15 ml) sesame oil

1 tbsp (15 ml) light soy sauce

½ tbsp (8 ml) dark soy sauce

¼ cup (60 ml) chicken broth

1 tsp cornstarch

¼ tsp sugar

¼ tsp white pepper

1 tbsp (15 ml) chili oil (optional)

For the Noodles

1 tbsp (15 ml) vegetable oil

2 tsp (3 g) minced garlic

2 tsp (3 g) minced ginger

1 cup (110 g) shredded carrots

1 cup (160 g) sliced onions

⅔ cup (32 g) sliced green onions

1½ cups (105 g) baby bok choy

1 lb (454 g) lo mein egg noodles (prepared according to package instructions)

1. To make the lo mein sauce, in a medium bowl, add the oyster sauce, sesame oil, light soy sauce, dark soy sauce, chicken broth, cornstarch, sugar, white pepper and chili oil. Mix until combined, and set aside.

2. In a wok or deep pan, heat up the vegetable oil. Once hot, add the minced garlic and ginger and sauté until fragrant. Add the carrots, onions and green onions and cook until tender. Add the baby bok choy and cook until wilted. Add the prepared egg noodles. Be sure they're not clumped together. If needed, you can run them under some warm water to break them apart.

3. Pour the lo mein sauce over the noodles and carefully stir to combine. Let everything cook together for 3 minutes, or until the sauce thickens, and then serve while hot!

CHIPOTLE CHICKEN AND CHARRED CORN TACOS

These tacos are the perfect Taco Tuesday meal. Made with intense, smoky and peppery flavors, these will surely liven up your weeknight. A soft tortilla hugs the juicy chicken, the creamy avocado and the slightly crunchy charred corn. Happy place unlocked.

Yield: 3 servings

1 lb (454 g) boneless chicken thigh or breast, diced into ½" (1.3-cm) taco-size bits

Juice of ½ lime

½ chipotle pepper, minced

2 tsp (10 ml) adobo sauce

1 tsp paprika

½ tsp smoked paprika

1 tsp cumin

1 tsp oregano

½ tsp chili powder

¼ tsp black pepper

1¼ tsp (4 g) garlic powder

1 tsp onion powder

Salt, to taste

2 tbsp (30 ml) olive oil, divided

1 cup (154 g) corn

For Serving

Tortillas, heated

Sliced avocado

Diced onions

Sour cream

Chopped cilantro

Salsa verde

1. In a bowl, add the diced chicken and mix with the lime juice, chipotle pepper, adobo sauce, paprika, smoked paprika, cumin, oregano, chili powder, pepper, garlic powder, onion powder and salt.

2. Heat a skillet over medium-high heat along with 1 tablespoon (15 ml) of the olive oil. Add the chicken and cook for 7 minutes, or until cooked through. Set aside and cover in foil.

3. Add the remaining oil to the skillet and turn the heat up to high. Once it gets very hot, add the corn and stir it around while scraping the bottom of the pan to release the charred and spiced flavors. Let the corn char for 2 to 3 minutes. Only mix it once or twice and don't over stir so that it can get a nice, charred color.

4. Assemble the chicken into heated tortillas, and then top with the charred corn, avocado, onions, sour cream, cilantro and salsa.

CHAPTER 2:
MIDDLE EASTERN
EATS *and*
FUSION TREATS

Okay, so being that I'm Middle Eastern and my passion lies in fusion foods, I may be slightly biased toward this chapter. When you love two cuisines, why not take the best flavors and ideas from each to make an even better dish? Not only do fusion foods explore new ways to enjoy the food we love, but they also bridge communities and spread the beauty of one culture to another. This chapter also shares some of my favorite classic Middle Eastern dishes that I grew up eating and are on a constant rotation in my home. Whether it be the Garlicky Chicken Shawarma Taquitos (page 47) or the classic Juicy Kafta Kebabs (page 51), the recipes ahead will have you constantly excited for your next meal!

SPICY SUJUK QUESADILLAS

I have been itching to share this one with you all. Sujuk is a dry sausage prominent in Turkey and the Middle East with a very flavorful filling of minced meat seasoned with garlic, cumin, dried peppers and other spices. In Syria, we have a sandwich we make of minced meat sautéed and seasoned with all the classic Sujuk flavors. This recipe bridges the Mexican crispy, cheesy quesadilla we all know and love with the extremely flavorful Sujuk mince. The garlic, cumin and pepper flavors pair perfectly with the quesadilla (think a Middle Eastern beef chorizo!).

Yield: 4 servings

1½ tbsp (23 ml) vegetable oil, divided

1 tsp crushed garlic

½ lb (226 g) 80% lean ground beef

1 tsp Aleppo pepper flakes (see Notes)

¾ tsp seven spice (see Notes)

¼ tsp black pepper

¾ tsp cumin

½ tsp dried coriander

¼ tsp ginger powder

¼ tsp nutmeg

½ tsp cloves

¾ tsp salt

½ tbsp (8 g) red pepper paste (see Notes)

½ tbsp (8 g) tomato paste

½ tbsp (8 ml) pomegranate molasses (see Notes)

1¾ cups (196 g) shredded mozzarella cheese

4 flour tortillas

1. Heat ½ tablespoon (8 ml) of the vegetable oil in a skillet over medium-high heat, and then add the crushed garlic. Sauté until fragrant, and then add the ground beef and begin to break it apart. Season with the Aleppo pepper flakes, seven spice, black pepper, cumin, coriander, ginger powder, nutmeg, cloves and salt.

2. Continue to break up the meat, and once it starts to brown, add the red pepper paste, tomato paste and pomegranate molasses. Cook for 2 minutes, or until the meat is fully cooked, and remove from the heat. Once the sujuk meat has cooled down, combine the meat with the shredded mozzarella in a bowl.

3. In a pan, heat the remaining oil over medium-high heat. Add a flour tortilla and heat it on one side for 1 minute, then flip it over. Sprinkle an even layer of the sujuk and cheese mixture onto the tortilla. Allow the bottom of the tortilla to crisp up and the cheese to melt. If needed, cover the pan with a lid to speed up the melting process. Once the tortilla is golden and crispy on the bottom and the cheese has melted, use a spatula to fold the tortilla over in half. Transfer to a cutting board and slice in half. Repeat this process with the remaining tortillas and filling and store in the fridge for an even quicker meal later.

Notes: Aleppo pepper flakes and seven spice can be found at any Middle Eastern market or online. Aleppo pepper flakes are slightly tangy and mildly spicy. If needed, you can substitute them with ½ teaspoon of red pepper flakes. If you can't find seven spice, feel free to substitute it with equal parts allspice.

Red pepper paste can be found in the canned and jarred goods section of any Middle Eastern market or online. You can choose mild or spicy, but for this recipe I do recommend the spicy one.

Pomegranate molasses is thick, tart and very slightly sweet. It's bottled and stored next to the olive oil at your local Middle Eastern market but can also be found online.

PITA NACHOS WITH RED PEPPER FETA DIP AND GARLIC ZA'ATAR LABNE

Move over, regular nachos, because these zesty, garlicky flavors are not here to play. The red pepper feta dip can best be described as a party in your mouth, and the garlic za'atar labne should slather itself onto everything I eat, please and thank you. Loaded up with Kalamata olives, pepperoncini, bell peppers, cucumbers and more, this treat will be your new weekly favorite.

Yield: 4 servings

For the Pita Chips
2 Greek pitas
½ tbsp (8 ml) olive oil
1 tsp za'atar
½ tsp dried oregano
¼ tsp garlic powder
¼ tsp sumac

For the Red Pepper Feta Dip
¾ cup (113 g) crumbled feta
½ tbsp (8 g) red pepper paste
½ tbsp (8 ml) olive oil
2½ tbsp (38 ml) labne (see Note)
¼ tsp black pepper
1 clove garlic, crushed
½ tbsp (8 ml) lemon juice

For the Garlic Za'atar Labne
1 cup (240 ml) labne (see Note)
¼ tsp salt
½ tbsp (4 g) crushed garlic
1 tsp Aleppo pepper flakes
½ tbsp (1 g) za'atar

For Serving
⅓ cup (49 g) quartered cherry tomatoes
⅓ cup (50 g) diced cucumber
⅓ cup (60 g) sliced Kalamata olives
⅓ cup (40 g) sliced pepperoncini
¼ cup (40 g) diced red onion
¼ cup (37 g) finely diced bell pepper

1. To make the pita chips, slice the Greek pitas into eighths. I use Greek pitas for this recipe because they're a bit thicker than the Middle Eastern ones and will hold all the dips and toppings better. Drizzle on the olive oil, and sprinkle on the za'atar, oregano, garlic powder and sumac. Toss until the pitas are evenly coated.

2. Air fry the pita chips at 360°F (180°C) for 5 minutes, and then flip and cook for 2 minutes more. The cook time will slightly vary depending on the air fryer being used so keep an eye out. You can also bake on a sheet tray at 400°F (200°C) for 7 minutes, flipping once halfway through. Set aside.

3. To make the feta dip, in a small bowl, add the feta, red pepper paste, olive oil, labne, pepper, crushed garlic and lemon juice. Mix until smooth and creamy and set aside.

4. For the za'atar labne, in a small bowl, mix together the labne, salt, crushed garlic, Aleppo pepper and za'atar.

5. Assemble the crispy pita chips on a large plate. Spoon a generous amount of the red pepper feta dip and garlic za'atar labne in the center. Sprinkle on the cherry tomatoes, cucumber, olives, sliced pepperoncini, red onion and bell pepper.

Note: Labne is a strained yogurt that is thicker than plain yogurt. It's a staple item in a Middle Eastern household and can be found in most local markets.

GARLICKY CHICKEN SHAWARMA TAQUITOS

This fusion between taquitos and chicken shawarma has been constantly requested since the first time I made it. Juicy, seasoned chicken filling, a drizzle of garlic mayo and diced Middle Eastern pickles for topping—yum! It has all the mouthwatering flavors of shawarma in the fun and addictive form of taquitos.

Yield: 4 servings

For the Garlic Mayonnaise

⅓ cup (80 ml) mayonnaise

1 tbsp (15 ml) lemon juice

½ tbsp (4 g) crushed garlic

¼ tsp salt, or to taste

For the Taquitos

3 cups (672 g) shredded rotisserie chicken

1 tsp allspice

½ tsp cumin

¼ tsp cardamom

½ tsp dried coriander

½ tsp onion powder

½ tsp garlic powder

½ tsp black pepper

1 tsp olive oil

½ tsp salt

3 tbsp (45 ml) chicken broth

12 corn tortillas

Vegetable oil, for cooking (optional)

Middle Eastern pickled cucumbers, diced (see Note)

Middle Eastern pickled turnips, diced (see Note)

1. To make the garlic mayo, in a small bowl, mix together the mayonnaise, lemon juice, crushed garlic and salt. Set aside.

2. To make the taquitos, in a large bowl, add the chicken, allspice, cumin, cardamom, coriander, onion powder, garlic powder, pepper, olive oil, salt and chicken broth. Mix until evenly combined.

3. Wrap the corn tortillas in a paper towel and microwave for 1 minute, or until they are soft and pliable. Add ¼ cup (56 g) of the chicken filling to each tortilla. Tightly roll the tortilla shut then brush oil on all sides. Place the taquitos seam side down in the air fryer basket. Repeat until the chicken filling has been used up.

4. Air fry at 390°F (200°C) for 9 minutes, or until crispy, flipping each taquito once halfway through. For a more traditional method, you can shallow fry these on all sides until golden. To do this, heat 1 inch (2.5 cm) of vegetable oil over medium-high heat in a pan and once hot, add the taquitos. Shallow fry on each side for 1 minute, or until crispy all around.

5. Plate the taquitos and drizzle on the garlic mayo. Top with the Middle Eastern pickled cucumber and turnips.

Note: Middle Eastern pickled cucumbers and turnips can be found at your local Middle Eastern market in the canned vegetables aisle.

SESAME HALLOUMI FRIES WITH ALEPPO HOT HONEY

Crispy sesame Halloumi fries dipped in an Aleppo pepper hot honey . . . this is what dreams are made of. I could go on and on about all the things I love about this: the crispiness from the sesame seeds, the saltiness of the cheese paired with the slightly spicy and sweet honey, etc., etc., etc.!

Yield: 4 servings

2 (8.8-oz [250-g]) packs Halloumi cheese

½ cup (63 g) all-purpose flour

2½ tsp (8 g) sesame seeds

½ tsp sumac

½ tsp za'atar

1 tsp dried oregano

¼ tsp black pepper

½ tsp smoked paprika

Oil, for frying

1 cup (240 ml) honey

3 dried red chile peppers

1 tsp Aleppo pepper flakes

1. Cut each block of the Halloumi into eight wedges. If your Halloumi came in a brine, it may be too salty, so soaking in cold water for at least 30 minutes, or longer if needed, will help.

2. On a plate, mix together the flour, sesame seeds, sumac, za'atar, oregano, pepper and smoked paprika. Evenly coat each wedge of Halloumi in the flour mixture.

3. Heat 1 inch (2.5 cm) of the oil in a shallow pan and fry the wedges on all sides until golden. If you choose to air fry them, cook at 375°F (190°C) for 11 minutes, or until golden, and flip once halfway through cooking.

4. For the hot honey, combine the honey, chile peppers and Aleppo pepper flakes in a saucepan. Let this come to a boil, and then simmer for 5 to 10 minutes. The longer it simmers, the spicier it'll be, so the simmer time is up to you! Strain the honey into a bowl and use it as a dipping sauce for the Halloumi wedges.

JUICY KAFTA KEBABS

This one hits home. Inspired by a family recipe, these incredibly juicy, flavorful and delicious kafta kebabs will elevate your weeknight dinner. Traditionally, these are grilled over charcoal, but for a quicker method, I prefer to bake them. These can be paired with a tangy salad, rice, yogurt, hummus and/or pita bread.

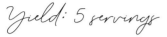

Yield: 5 servings

1 onion, quartered

1 bunch parsley

½ –1 whole jalapeño (depending on spice preference)

2 lb (907 g) 80% lean ground beef

½ cup (68 g) pine nuts

1 tsp black pepper

2½ tsp (5 g) seven spice

½ tbsp (3 g) allspice

2 tsp (12 g) salt, or more as desired

Tangy salad, for serving

Hummus, for serving

Pita bread, for serving

1. Preheat the oven to 400°F (200°C). Line a baking sheet with aluminum foil.

2. Pulse the onion, parsley and jalapeño in a food processor until very finely chopped. (These can also be hand chopped if you don't have a food processor.)

3. In a bowl, add the onion, jalapeño and parsley mixture with the ground beef, pine nuts, pepper, seven spice, allspice and salt. Mix well and form 3- to 4-inch (8- to 10-cm) mini-kebab logs. Assemble them with ½ inch (1.3 cm) of spacing between them on the baking sheet.

4. Bake for 15 minutes, or until cooked to your liking. Serve with a tangy chopped salad, hummus and pita bread.

Note: If cooking on a grill, soak the wooden skewers in water for 30 minutes to prevent burning. Form the kebabs around the skewers, and then add them to the hot grill over medium heat. Once the bottom side has firmed up after about 4 minutes, rotate the kebabs and cook the other side through for another 4 to 5 minutes.

MY FAVORITE ZESTY ORZO SALAD

This Greek orzo salad is my weakness. The tangy flavors and the chewy orzo with the fresh, crisp veggies and creamy feta . . . it's truly an experience to eat. This salad is great for meal prep because the flavors taste better with each passing day. It's also delicious paired with grilled shrimp or chicken skewers.

Yield: 4 servings

1 cup (220 g) uncooked orzo

1¼ cups (180 g) sliced cucumber

1 cup (149 g) sliced cherry tomatoes

1 cup (180 g) sliced Kalamata olives

½ cup (80 g) diced red onions

½ cup (27 g) sliced sun-dried tomatoes

1 cup (150 g) crumbled feta

1 tbsp (9 g) crushed garlic

Juice of 1 large lemon, or to taste

2 tbsp (30 ml) olive oil

1 tbsp (5 g) dried oregano

1 tsp black pepper

1 tsp crushed red pepper flakes (optional)

Salt, to taste

1. Add the orzo to salted boiling water and cook for 6 minutes. Strain, rinse, and then allow the orzo to cool in a salad bowl.

2. Top the orzo with the cucumber, cherry tomatoes, olives, onions, sun-dried tomatoes, feta, garlic, lemon juice, olive oil, oregano, pepper, red pepper flakes (if using) and salt. Mix and enjoy.

BEEF SHAWARMA AND YELLOW RICE

Eating beef shawarma always takes me back to the bustling streets of Damascus, Syria. The juicy, tender steak is seasoned to perfection and goes so well with the fluffy yellow rice. Try this delicious meal to switch up your weeknight routine.

Yield: 4 servings

For the Yellow Rice

½ tbsp (7 g) butter

2 cups (400 g) uncooked medium-grain rice

3 cups (720 ml) chicken broth

1 tsp garlic powder

½ tsp cumin

1 tsp salt

¼ tsp black pepper

½ tsp turmeric

½ tsp allspice

½ tsp onion powder

1 tsp low-sodium Maggi Chicken Seasoning (optional)

1 bay leaf

For the Beef Shawarma

2 boneless ribeye steaks

½ tsp black pepper

1 tsp seven spice

1 tsp allspice

1 tsp dried coriander

1 tsp garlic powder

1 tsp onion powder

¼ tsp dried ginger

¾ tsp cumin

¾ tsp lemon pepper

¼ tsp cinnamon

1 tsp salt

1½ tbsp (23 ml) olive oil

1 tsp vinegar

For Serving

Hummus

Zesty salad

1. To make the rice, melt the butter over medium-high heat in a pot. Add the rice and toast for 2 to 3 minutes. Pour in the chicken broth and season with the garlic powder, cumin, salt, pepper, turmeric, allspice, onion powder, Maggi seasoning (if using) and bay leaf. Bring it to a boil, and then lower the heat to its lowest setting and cover with a lid. Cook the rice for about 17 minutes, remove the bay leaf and then fluff with a fork once ready.

2. To make the beef shawarma, slice the steak into very thin, ¾-inch (2-cm)-thick bits. Prepare the spice mix by mixing the pepper, seven spice, allspice, coriander, garlic powder, onion powder, ginger, cumin, lemon pepper, cinnamon and salt together in a small bowl.

3. Heat the olive oil in a skillet over high heat. Once hot, add the steak with the spices and vinegar and cook for 6 to 8 minutes. Once the steak is browned and the juices in the pan have started to dry, remove from the heat.

4. Serve the beef shawarma with the fluffy yellow rice, hummus and a zesty salad.

LOADED EGGPLANT WRAPS

These crispy eggplant sandwiches are filled with flavor and fresh, crisp veggies. It is easily my favorite sandwich. When even your meat-loving husband says he doesn't miss the meat and can eat this all the time, you know it's a pretty big win. If you're not a fan of eggplant, try this same sandwich using cauliflower or potatoes—the flavors are amazing!

Yield: 5 servings

2 cups (480 ml) plain yogurt

1 tbsp (15 ml) lemon juice

½ tsp salt

1 tsp pomegranate molasses

1 tbsp (8 g) crushed garlic

1 tsp tahini

2 large eggplants

Salt, to taste

¼ tsp black pepper

Vegetable oil, for frying

5 pieces pita bread

For Serving

Mint leaves

Thinly sliced tomato

Thinly sliced pickles

Thinly sliced lemon

Thinly sliced red onion

Pickled turnips

Thinly sliced radishes

Sumac, to taste

Hot sauce (optional)

1. In a medium bowl, mix together the yogurt, lemon juice, salt, pomegranate molasses, crushed garlic and tahini. Set aside.

2. Peel the eggplant skin into strips. Slice the eggplant, lengthwise into thin, ¼-inch (6-mm) strips. Season both sides of the eggplant with salt and pepper.

3. Heat 1 inch (2.5 cm) of the vegetable oil in a frying pan. Place the long, sliced eggplant pieces in the oil and fry until crispy and golden on both sides, about 1 to 2 minutes per side. Remove the eggplant and place it on a cooling rack so that it remains crispy.

4. Assemble the wrap by spreading the yogurt sauce onto the pita bread and layer on the eggplant, mint, tomato, pickles, lemon slices, onion, turnips, and radishes, and then top with a dash of sumac and hot sauce (if using).

BATATA HARRA (GARLIC RED PEPPER POTATOES)

This dish is constantly requested in my home. Crispy, fried potatoes are coated in garlic, red pepper, cilantro and lemon sauce. The potatoes soak up the garlicky lemony goodness and will have you so satisfied, not even a Saturday night out can compete. But I warn you: After making this once for your friends or family, you'll find yourself making it all the time to keep up with the requests. Yes, it's that good!

Yield: 4 servings

Oil, for cooking

4½ cups (675 g) diced potatoes (½" x ½" [1.3 x 1.3 cm])

Salt, to taste

3 tbsp (45 ml) olive oil

¼ cup (34 g) crushed garlic

2 tsp (10 g) red pepper paste

½ tsp crushed red pepper flakes

3 tbsp (45 ml) lemon juice

1 bunch cilantro, finely chopped

Pita bread, for serving

1. Heat 1½ inches (4 cm) of the oil in a frying pan. Season the diced potatoes with salt. Once the oil is hot, add the diced potatoes and fry for about 13 minutes, or until golden.

2. Heat the olive oil in a separate pan over medium-high heat. Add the garlic and sauté until fragrant. Add the red pepper paste and crushed red pepper flakes and sauté for 2 minutes. Mix in the lemon juice and salt to taste. Turn off the heat and stir in the cilantro.

3. Add the crispy diced potatoes to the garlic red pepper mixture and gently toss together until the potatoes are evenly coated. Serve with the pita bread to scoop it all up and enjoy!

KAFTA AND CHEESE PIZZA

This slight twist on a Middle Eastern classic, kafta and cheese manaeesh, is everything you're missing in your life. The crispy, chewy pizza dough perfectly supports the juicy, flavorful meat mixture. The salty cheese blankets it all and provides you with that satisfying cheese pull with each bite. Topped with fresh vegetables, herbs and a drizzle of tahini pomegranate sauce, this pizza is one for the books (literally!).

Yield: 3 (8" [20-cm]) pizzas

½ onion, quartered

½ bunch parsley

1 lb (454 g) ground beef

½ tsp black pepper

1¼ tsp (6 g) seven spice

¾ tsp allspice

Salt, as desired

3 (8" [20-cm]) prepared thin-crust pizza crusts (I use the Boboli Original Thin Pizza Crust found in most local grocery stores)

3 cups (336 g) shredded mozzarella cheese

¼ cup (60 ml) plain yogurt

1 tsp tahini

½ tsp pomegranate molasses

¼ red onion, thinly sliced

⅓ cup (49 g) sliced cherry tomatoes

1 cup (94 g) arugula or fresh mint leaves

1. Preheat the oven to 450°F (230°C).

2. Pulse the onion and parsley in a food processor until very finely chopped. (These can also be hand chopped if you don't have a food processor.) In a bowl, mix together the onion and parsley with the ground beef, pepper, seven spice, allspice and salt.

3. Separate the meat mixture into three equal parts. Using your hands, evenly spread one-third of the mixture onto one pizza crust in a thin layer. (If your pizza crust is larger or smaller, adjust the ratio to your appropriate size. A large pizza may use the entire meat mixture.) Repeat with the remaining crusts. Sprinkle on the cheese.

4. Bake each crust (with or without a pizza tray) for 8 to 10 minutes, or until the crust is golden and the cheese has melted.

5. While the pizzas are cooking, prepare the tahini sauce by mixing together in a small bowl the yogurt, tahini, pomegranate molasses and salt. Top the finished pizza with the red onions, cherry tomatoes, arugula or mint and a drizzle of the tahini sauce. Serve hot!

CHAPTER 3:
NUTRITIOUS
Meets DELICIOUS

If you're looking for quick, healthy and flavorful dishes that'll make your Monday feel like a Saturday night, this chapter is for you! I often get messages requesting healthy recipes because folks are "so sick of eating the same baked chicken and salad." This chapter will show you that there is such a large variety of foods you can make when trying to eat clean. It really doesn't have to be redundant and bland! The recipes in this chapter are lighter than the rest and focus on nutritious, wholesome meals that are fun and loaded with different spices, herbs and flavors. Let's jump in!

ASIAN CHICKEN LETTUCE WRAPS

Refreshing, quick, healthy and downright delicious, these chicken wraps are my go-to meal when I need something light and flavorful. This chicken mixture is extremely versatile—you can use it in lettuce wraps, as an eggroll filling or with steamed rice and vegetables.

Yield: 3 servings

1 tbsp (15 ml) vegetable oil

1 tbsp (8 g) crushed garlic

1 tsp minced ginger

½ cup (80 g) diced onion

½ cup (70 g) strained canned diced water chestnuts

1 lb (454 g) ground chicken breast

1½ tbsp (23 ml) soy sauce

2 tsp (10 ml) sesame oil

1 tsp rice vinegar

2 tsp (10 ml) sriracha

1 tbsp (15 ml) honey

5 tbsp (75 ml) hoisin sauce

Butter lettuce leaves

Sliced scallions, for garnishing

1. Heat the vegetable oil in a pan over medium-high heat. Add the garlic, ginger and onion and sauté until fragrant. Add the water chestnuts, chicken, soy sauce, sesame oil and rice vinegar. Toss together while breaking the chicken apart. Cook for 5 minutes as you continue to break apart the chicken. Stir in the sriracha, honey and hoisin sauce and cook for 3 to 5 minutes.

2. Arrange the lettuce leaves on a platter and spoon ¼ cup (57 g) of the chicken filling into each leaf. Garnish with sliced scallions.

MOROCCAN SPICED CAULIFLOWER STEAKS

Fun, different and absolutely delicious, these cauliflower steaks are seasoned to perfection and will introduce a new favorite meal to your dinner table. Growing up, I always loved when my mother would fry cauliflower florets. We'd season them, and then squeeze a generous amount of lemon juice on top after they were golden and crispy. Here is a fun, lighter version that is baked instead of deep-fried. The Moroccan-inspired flavors work so well on the crispy, roasted cauliflower. I highly recommend a light drizzle of pomegranate molasses and tahini on top of these to absolutely blow your taste buds away!

Yield: 3 servings

1 head cauliflower

¼ cup (60 ml) olive oil

2 tbsp (30 ml) lemon juice, plus more for garnishing

½ tbsp (3 g) cumin

½ tsp black pepper

½ tsp turmeric

½ tsp smoked paprika

½ tsp allspice

½ tsp dried coriander

1 tsp garlic powder

1 tsp paprika

Salt, to taste

Pomegranate molasses, for garnishing (optional)

Tahini, for garnishing (optional)

1 tbsp (4 g) chopped parsley, for garnishing

1. Preheat the oven to 425°F (220°C). Line a large baking sheet with foil.

2. Wash the cauliflower head, and then trim off the outer green leaves. Rest the head on its stem, and then slice it from top to bottom, creating ¾-inch (2-cm) cauliflower steaks. Arrange the cauliflower steaks in a single layer—along with any florets that may have crumbled loose—onto the baking sheet. Set aside.

3. In a bowl, add the olive oil, lemon juice, cumin, pepper, turmeric, smoked paprika, allspice, coriander, garlic powder, paprika and salt. Mix well, and then drizzle half the sauce onto the cauliflower steaks. Rub it into the cauliflower so that every part is covered, and then flip over the steaks and drizzle the remaining half of the sauce onto the other side and rub that in as well.

4. Bake the cauliflower in the middle oven rack for 10 minutes, and then carefully flip the steaks over and bake for 10 to 15 minutes, or until the cauliflower is golden and roasted. I like to garnish it with a light drizzle of pomegranate molasses, tahini, chopped parsley and a squeeze of lemon juice.

Note: Naturally, some florets will crumble off as you slice the cauliflower. If you want more than four guaranteed cauliflower steaks, I recommend doubling this recipe!

THAI YELLOW CURRY NOODLE SOUP

I can never get enough of this creamy soup. It's so simple to make, it's completely vegan for a lighter option and the flavors are incredible. This recipe is nostalgic to me because it's one of the first meals I whipped up when my husband and I moved in together, and since then, it's a regular in our home. This dish is not your average noodle soup as it'll satisfy any noodle *and* curry cravings at the same time!

Yield: 4 servings

1 tbsp (15 ml) olive oil

1 tbsp (8 g) grated ginger

1 tbsp (8 g) minced garlic

4 cups (960 ml) vegetable broth

3 tbsp (48 g) Thai yellow curry paste

1½ cups (360 ml) coconut milk

1 tbsp (3 g) chopped fresh basil

1 tbsp (1 g) chopped cilantro

Juice of 1 lime, plus more for serving (optional)

½ tbsp (4 g) garlic powder

¼ tsp black pepper

Salt, to taste

½ lb (226 g) uncooked vermicelli noodles

Sliced jalapeños, for garnishing (optional)

1. Heat the olive oil in a pot over medium-high heat. Once the oil is hot, add the ginger and garlic and cook for 1 minute, or until fragrant. Pour in the vegetable broth and yellow curry paste. Stir until the curry paste has completely dissolved and no clumps remain.

2. Let the soup boil for 5 minutes. Reduce the heat to medium and stir in the coconut milk. Simmer for 5 minutes, and then add in the basil, cilantro, lime juice, garlic powder, pepper, salt and noodles. Cook for 5 minutes, or until the noodles are cooked al dente. Top with sliced jalapeños for a touch of heat (optional) and a squeeze of lime juice, if desired.

TANGY ZA'ATAR CHICKEN SKEWERS

You can never go wrong with chicken skewers, and I promise these tangy za'atar ones will blow you away. If you're unfamiliar with za'atar, it's a mixture of dried oregano and/or thyme, toasted sesame seeds, sumac, salt and other spices. It can easily be found at any Middle Eastern market or online. Growing up, it was common for my Middle Eastern family to eat chicken kebabs and to eat za'atar with bread, but never za'atar and chicken kebabs together. This recipe combines some of my favorite flavors with the classic chicken kebab.

Yield: 3 servings

¼ cup (60 ml) olive oil
¼ cup (60 ml) lemon juice
1 tbsp (15 ml) za'atar (see Note)
1 tsp sumac (see Note)
1 tsp garlic powder
½ tsp black pepper
½ tsp salt, or to taste
1½ lb (680 g) boneless, skinless chicken breast

1. Preheat the oven to 450°F (230°C). If using wooden skewers, soak them in water for at least 15 minutes to prevent burning. Line a baking sheet with aluminum foil.

2. In a bowl, mix together the olive oil, lemon juice, za'atar, sumac, garlic powder, pepper and salt. Taste the marinade and adjust the salt to your liking because each za'atar mix has varying levels of salt.

3. Prepare the chicken by cutting it into 1-inch (2.5-cm) cubes. Add the cubes to the prepared marinade and mix until fully coated. If you have time, let this marinate for as long as you can. Preparing the chicken the night before and marinating overnight yields the best results but is not necessary.

4. Pierce the marinated chicken onto the skewers. Thread onto the skewer so that the edges of each piece of chicken are barely touching, and be sure not to squish them together so that the chicken cooks evenly. Leave 1 inch (2.5 cm) on both ends of the skewers empty and wrap them with foil.

5. Arrange the chicken skewers in a single layer onto the baking sheet. Bake on the middle oven rack for 10 minutes, and then flip and bake for another 10 minutes, or until cooked through. Serve with your choice of salad, rice, hummus or roasted vegetables.

Note: Za'atar and sumac can both be found at your local Middle Eastern grocery store or online. Sumac is a berry from a flowering plant that is dried and coarsely ground. It is red-purple in color and brings a very lemony, tart flavor to your food.

TERIYAKI GLAZED SALMON

This salmon is tender, flavorful and simple to make. The sweet and tangy flavors are perfectly balanced in this homemade teriyaki sauce. The salmon takes minutes to cook and is delicious when paired with white rice and steamed vegetables. My husband ranks this dish in his top-three favorite meals, so this one is always a winner in my home.

Yield: 4 servings

1 tbsp (8 g) crushed garlic

1 tsp minced ginger

¼ cup (60 ml) soy sauce

3 tbsp (42 g) brown sugar

1 tbsp (15 ml) sesame oil

1 tbsp (15 ml) rice vinegar

1 tbsp (15 ml) honey

4 skinless salmon fillets

1 tsp cornstarch

1 tbsp (15 ml) water

2 tbsp (30 ml) hoisin sauce

1 tbsp (15 ml) vegetable oil

2 scallions, thinly sliced, for garnishing

½ tsp toasted sesame seeds, for garnishing

1. In a bowl, mix together the garlic, ginger, soy sauce, brown sugar, sesame oil, rice vinegar and honey. Pour half of the sauce into a small saucepan and set aside.

2. Add the salmon fillets to the remaining half of the sauce in the bowl and mix until fully coated. Set aside to marinate. If you have time to prepare this a few hours in advance so the salmon can marinate for longer, it will yield even better results!

3. Heat the reserved sauce in the saucepan over medium heat until it starts to simmer. In a small bowl, mix together the cornstarch and water to create a cornstarch slurry. Slowly mix this into the simmering sauce along with the hoisin sauce. Let this simmer over medium-low now for 5 minutes, or until the sauce has thickened and coats the back of a spoon.

4. Meanwhile, pour the vegetable oil in a cast-iron or large skillet over medium-high heat, and once hot, add the salmon. Be sure not to overcrowd the skillet and cook in separate batches if needed. Cook the salmon on one side for 3 minutes, and then flip and reduce the heat to medium and cook for 4 minutes, or until cooked to your liking.

5. Generously spoon the sauce onto the salmon fillets and garnish with sliced scallions and toasted sesame seeds.

SPICED BEEF KEEMA

Keema is a South Asian dish that literally translates to "minced or ground meat." It can be made with ground chicken, beef, goat, lamb, etc. There are several variations of the dish, and you'll find that no two people make it exactly alike . . . whether it be a different type of meat used; different vegetables added; more, less or different spices used; etc. I've been making this for ten years now, tweaking and adding ingredients until it was perfect. This final recipe is a personal favorite and has won the heart of so many who try it. It's delicious when paired with some basmati rice or garlic naan.

Yield: 6 servings

½ tsp turmeric

1 tbsp (6 g) chili powder

½ tbsp (3 g) dried coriander

2½ tsp (5 g) garam masala

2 tsp (6 g) paprika

½ tsp ground cloves

2 tsp (4 g) black pepper

½ tsp ground cardamom

2 tsp (4 g) cumin

¼ tsp cinnamon

¼ tsp cayenne, for an extra kick of spice (optional)

2 tsp (12 g) salt, or to taste

1 tbsp (15 ml) olive oil

1 large onion, finely diced

1 jalapeño, finely diced (or more or less depending on spice preference)

2½ tbsp (38 g) garlic ginger paste (see Notes)

2 lb (907 g) ground beef or chicken

1½ cups (270 g) diced tomatoes

1½ cups (225 g) diced potatoes (optional; see Notes)

1 cup (145 g) peas (optional; see Notes)

Juice of ½ lime

3 tbsp (3 g) finely chopped cilantro

1½ tbsp (9 g) finely chopped mint leaves

Basmati rice, for serving

Naan, for serving

1. In a medium bowl, mix together the turmeric, chili powder, coriander, garam masala, paprika, cloves, pepper, cardamom, cumin, cinnamon, cayenne (if using) and salt. Set aside.

2. Heat the olive oil in a saucepan over medium-high heat. Add the onion and jalapeño. Sauté for 2 minutes, and then add the garlic ginger paste and sauté for 1 minute.

3. Add the ground meat with half of the spice mixture and fully break up the meat. Cook for 5 minutes, or until the meat is no longer pink, and then mix in the diced tomatoes, potatoes (if using) and the other half of the spice mix.

4. Lower the heat to medium-low, cover the pot with the lid, and cook for 12 minutes, or until the potatoes are cooked. Uncover and add the peas (if using), lime juice, cilantro and mint and simmer for 2 to 3 minutes. Serve with plain basmati rice or naan for an unforgettable meal!

Notes: Garlic ginger paste can be found in most grocery stores, but if you're unable to find any, you can substitute it with 1½ tablespoons (12 g) of crushed garlic and 1 tablespoon (8 g) of grated ginger.

The potatoes and peas are listed as optional because, as mentioned before, there are so many different ways to make this dish. I prefer to add both, but I don't always if I want an even quicker or lower-carb dish. If leaving out the potatoes and peas, I like to double the diced tomatoes and cut the covered cooking time of 12 minutes down to 6 minutes. When adding in the cilantro, mint and lime juice sans the peas, only cook for 1 minute, and then serve.

SESAME GINGER CHICKEN SALAD

Simply put, this is one of my all-time favorite salads. Many years ago, I ordered a Chinese chicken salad at a small shop, and I fell in love. I went home and tried to recreate it, and it turned out even better. This version has more flavor and balance of acidity and sweetness in the dressing, along with an extra crunch of ingredients. About a year later, I went back to the restaurant, and I no longer loved the salad after having had my version all year. It's sweet, nutty, gingery and just so refreshing and delicious.

Yield: 2 servings

For the Dressing

1½ tbsp (23 ml) soy sauce

1½ tbsp (23 ml) sesame oil

2 tsp (10 ml) rice vinegar

1½ tbsp (23 ml) honey

½ tbsp (5 g) toasted sesame seeds

¾ tsp grated ginger

1 tsp minced garlic

For the Salad

1 head romaine lettuce, finely chopped

⅓ cup (37 g) shredded carrots

¼ cup (60 g) sliced pickled ginger (shoestring size)

⅓ cup (19 g) chow mein noodles (I prefer La Choy)

1 cooked chicken breast (rotisserie, steamed, baked, etc.), sliced

½ avocado, thinly sliced

2 scallions, thinly sliced

⅓ cup (36 g) thinly sliced toasted almonds

¼ cup (4 g) chopped cilantro

1 mandarin orange or 1 cup (244 g) drained jarred mandarin oranges (optional but highly recommended)

1. To make the dressing, in a bowl, mix together the soy sauce, sesame oil, rice vinegar, honey, sesame seeds, ginger and garlic. Set aside.

2. In a salad bowl, combine the lettuce, carrots, pickled ginger, noodles, chicken breast, avocado, scallions, toasted almonds, cilantro and mandarin (if using). Drizzle on the sesame dressing and give the salad a light toss. Serve while fresh!

MY FAMOUS FLAVOR BOMB SALMON

This is the first salmon dish (and the only one of two in this book [see page 73]) that has ever won my heart. I named it Flavor Bomb Salmon because the flavors here are that intense, and I absolutely love it. This is one of my top favorite recipes, and I'll be honest, I'm not usually a fan of fish. I tasted so many versions throughout the years, and I personally just couldn't get into it. Then a few years ago, my mother made me salmon with fresh garlic, ginger, lemon pepper and Cajun seasoning, and I actually enjoyed it. This was a huge deal for me, so I took some of those flavors, added many more and created my all-time favorite seafood recipe. This is delicious served with rice, roasted potatoes, roasted carrots, broccoli or a fresh salad.

Yield: 6 servings

3½ tbsp (53 ml) olive oil

10 cloves garlic, finely chopped

1½ tsp (5 g) grated ginger

¼ cup (60 ml) lemon juice

1 tsp lemon zest

1 tbsp (6 g) Cajun seasoning

1 tsp paprika

1 tbsp (16 g) red pepper paste (see Note)

1 tsp cumin

1 tsp sumac (see Note)

½ tsp black pepper

Salt, to taste

1 side of salmon (boneless, skin on or off, depending on your preference)

Chopped parsley, for garnishing

1. Preheat the oven to 400°F (200°C). Line a large baking sheet with an extra-long sheet of aluminum foil, enough to wrap the whole salmon in later on.

2. In a medium bowl, combine the olive oil, garlic, ginger, lemon juice, lemon zest, Cajun seasoning, paprika, red pepper paste, cumin, sumac, pepper and salt to form the marinade.

3. Place the salmon on the baking sheet with the bottom side facing up, and spread a layer of the marinade onto it. Flip the salmon over and spread a very generous amount of marinade on top, creating a thick coat.

4. Fold the foil over and pinch all the edges shut to completely cover the salmon, and bake it in the oven for 15 to 20 minutes. (Cook time will vary depending on the thickness of your salmon.) Uncover the salmon and broil for 2 to 3 minutes. Garnish with chopped parsley.

Note: Red pepper paste and sumac can both be found at your local Middle Eastern market and online. I highly recommend using them, but if you're unable to, you may leave them out as the recipe will still be delicious.

KOREAN BEEF BOWLS

This meal is on a constant rotation in my home. It takes about twenty minutes to make and always hits the spot. The sweet, spicy and nutty flavors work so well together with the browned beef. Serve it with some white rice and steamed vegetables and you have yourself a delicious and healthy meal!

Yield: 3 servings

1 tbsp (15 ml) vegetable oil

½ onion, finely diced

1 tbsp (8 g) minced garlic

1 tsp grated ginger

1 scallion, thinly sliced, plus more for garnishing

1 lb (454 g) ground beef

1 tbsp (15 ml) sesame oil

1 tbsp (15 ml) hoisin sauce

1 tbsp (15 ml) honey

2 tbsp (30 ml) soy sauce

¼ tsp salt

¼ tsp white pepper

½ tsp rice vinegar

½ tsp sriracha

½ tsp crushed red pepper flakes (add more or less depending on spice preference)

Toasted sesame seeds, for garnishing

Cooked white or brown rice, for serving

Steamed vegetables, for serving

1. Heat the vegetable oil in a saucepan over medium-high heat. Add the onion, garlic, ginger and scallion and sauté for 2 minutes, or until softened. Add the ground beef and break it up for 1 minute.

2. Add the sesame oil, hoisin sauce, honey, soy sauce, salt, white pepper, rice vinegar, sriracha and red pepper flakes. Stir as you continue to break the meat down finely. Cook for 5 minutes, or until the meat is no longer pink. Top it with scallions and toasted sesame seeds and serve over rice or with steamed veggies.

BASIL LEMON MEATBALLS

These meatballs are as easy as they are delicious. My favorite part is that they're so versatile that we've enjoyed them with pasta, in subs, in a Greek pita, with salad, with rice, etc. These meatballs are made low-carb by using ricotta cheese instead of bread crumbs, making them keto friendly.

Yield: 3 servings

1 lb (454 g) ground chicken (thigh or breast will both work, but thigh is much juicier)

1 tbsp (3 g) finely chopped basil

1 tbsp (15 ml) lemon juice

2 tsp (4 g) lemon zest

¼ cup (62 g) ricotta cheese

1 tsp salt

½ tsp black pepper

¾ tsp garlic powder

¾ tsp dried thyme

1. Preheat the oven to 400°F (200°C). Lightly grease a foil-lined baking sheet with cooking spray.

2. In a bowl, add the ground chicken, basil, lemon juice, lemon zest, ricotta, salt, pepper, garlic powder and thyme. Mix well, and then slightly wet your hands to form about 22 golf ball–sized meatballs

3. Evenly assemble the meatballs onto the baking sheet. Bake in the middle rack for 20 minutes, or until the center of the meatballs read 165°F (75°C) with an instant-read thermometer.

STICKY HONEY GARLIC SHRIMP

This is the perfect dish to make for a weeknight dinner as it only takes about fifteen minutes and most of the ingredients are likely already in your pantry. This saucy shrimp has the perfect amount of garlic and honey, as well as a kick of ginger and spice. It'll satisfy any takeout cravings and is healthier and much more delicious.

Yield: 2 servings

¼ cup (60 ml) soy sauce

8 cloves garlic, finely chopped

½ tsp ginger powder

¼ tsp white pepper

7 tbsp (105 ml) honey

1 tbsp (15 g) sambal chili paste (optional)

1 tbsp (15 ml) vegetable oil

1 lb (454 g) jumbo shrimp, peeled and deveined, tails off

1 tsp cornstarch

2 tsp (10 ml) water

2 scallions, thinly sliced

½ tsp toasted sesame seeds

1. In a bowl, whisk together the soy sauce, garlic, ginger powder, white pepper, honey and chili paste (if using), and then set aside.

2. Heat the vegetable oil in a pan over medium-high heat. Once the oil is hot, add the shrimp and cook for 1 minute on each side, or until pink. We just want to get some color on the shrimp here—it doesn't need to be fully cooked on the inside just yet!

3. Remove the shrimp from the pan and set aside. Pour the prepared sauce into the pan, and let it come to a simmer over medium heat.

4. In a small bowl, evenly mix together the cornstarch and water to create a cornstarch slurry. Slowly mix this into the heated sauce, and let it all simmer together for 3 to 5 minutes, or until you have a thick, sticky sauce.

5. Toss the shrimp back into the pan. Cook together for about 3 minutes, or until the shrimp is fully cooked. Garnish with the sliced scallions and toasted sesame seeds.

SIZZLING CHILI SHRIMP FAJITAS

These fajitas are a family favorite. The flavors of the garlic, onion, bell peppers and smoky spices paired with a splash of pineapple juice to balance it all out create the most amazing fajitas I've ever had! This dish is naturally low-carb and is delicious when eaten on its own, but if you're watching the carb intake and are itching for a tortilla, low-carb tortillas work great here.

Yield: 3 servings

½ red bell pepper

1 green bell pepper

1 onion

¼ cup (60 ml) pineapple juice

3 tbsp (45 ml) lemon juice

1½ tbsp (23 ml) adobo sauce

½ tbsp (4 g) garlic powder

½ tbsp (3 g) paprika

1 tsp smoked paprika

1 tsp chili powder

½ tbsp (3 g) cumin

1 tsp onion powder

½ tsp black pepper, plus more to taste

¾ tsp salt, plus more to taste

¼ cup (60 ml) olive oil, divided

1½ lb (680 g) jumbo shrimp, peeled and deveined, tails off

½ bunch cilantro, finely chopped, for garnishing

For Serving
Warm tortillas

Rice

Salsa

Limes

Sour cream

Diced onions

Avocado slices or guacamole

Crumbled queso fresco

1. Slice the red bell pepper, green bell pepper and onion into ½-inch (1.3-cm)-wide slices. You don't want to slice these too thin, because otherwise they get soggy!

2. In a bowl, add the pineapple juice, lemon juice, adobo sauce, garlic powder, paprika, smoked paprika, chili powder, cumin, onion powder, pepper, salt and 2 tablespoons (30 ml) of the olive oil. Mix well, and then add the jumbo shrimp and let this marinate for 10 minutes. Be sure not to marinate for any longer than that or the acidity will start to cook the shrimp through!

3. Heat 1 tablespoon (15 ml) of the olive oil in a skillet over high heat, and once the pan gets hot, add the bell peppers and onions. Leave them to slightly char on each side for 2 minutes before stirring. Stir and then allow them to char again for 2 minutes. Then, stir once more. In total, they should be cooked for 5 minutes, or until they're lightly charred on the edges and slightly softened. Season the vegetables with salt and pepper, and then remove them from the skillet and onto a plate and set aside.

4. In the same skillet, heat up the remaining olive oil over medium-high heat. Using tongs, drip off the excess marinade on the shrimp one by one and place in the sizzling pan. Cook the shrimp on each side for 2 minutes, or until the shrimp turns pink. Toss the sautéed vegetables back in and garnish with the cilantro. Serve immediately with flour tortillas and your favorite fajita sides!

AVOCADO LIME CHICKEN TACOS

Because who doesn't love a flavorful taco? Super seasoned, smoky chicken with the slight tang of creamy guacamole paired with all your favorite taco fixings . . . these are pure perfection. These tacos never fail to leave everyone satisfied and raving about the meal. I'll be honest, we eat these more than once a week at times, and we never get sick of them!

Yield: 4 servings

For the Quick Guacamole

2 avocados

Juice of 1½ limes

½ tsp minced garlic

¼ tsp crushed red pepper flakes

¼ tsp black pepper

Salt, to taste

For the Chicken

1 lb (454 g) chicken breast

1 tbsp (15 ml) olive oil

1 tsp cumin

1 tsp paprika

1 tsp chili powder

1 tsp dried oregano

1 tsp garlic powder

1 tsp onion powder

½ tsp black pepper

1 tsp salt, or to taste

1 tbsp (15 ml) lime juice

For Serving

Mini corn or flour street taco tortillas, heated

Diced onions

Chopped cilantro

Chopped cherry tomatoes

Salsa

Limes wedges

1. Prepare the quick guacamole by mashing together in a medium bowl, the avocados, lime juice, garlic, red pepper flakes, pepper and salt until smooth and creamy. Set aside.

2. To make the chicken, dice it into small, taco-size cubes. Heat the oil in a skillet and once it's hot, add the chicken. Stir to cook and season with the cumin, paprika, chili powder, oregano, garlic powder, onion powder, pepper and salt. Cook the chicken for 7 minutes, or until it's fully cooked. Stir in the lime juice, and then remove from the heat.

3. Assemble your heated tortillas onto a platter and spread a generous spoonful of guacamole onto each tortilla. Then, add a heaping spoonful of the hot chicken. Garnish with onions, cilantro, cherry tomatoes, your favorite salsa and lime wedges.

GARLIC HERB STEAK AND POTATO SKILLET

Personally, I've never seen a better pair than steak and potatoes. They look good, they taste good and they'll never do you dirty. Every time I whip up this recipe, I'm amazed at how a meal this good can come together so quickly. It may be a weeknight, but this will make you feel like you're dining out on a Saturday night.

Yield: 3 servings

2½ cups (375 g) halved Yukon Gold baby potatoes

1½ lb (680 g) boneless steak (use your favorite cut—I like using ribeye or filet mignon!)

1 tsp black pepper, divided, plus more as needed

1 tsp salt, divided, plus more as needed

½ tsp garlic powder, divided

1½ tbsp (23 ml) Worcestershire sauce

¼ cup (57 g) unsalted butter, divided

2 tsp (3 g) chopped fresh rosemary

1 tbsp (8 g) crushed garlic

2 tbsp (8 g) chopped parsley, for garnishing

1. Add the halved gold baby potatoes to a pot filled with enough water to cover the potatoes. Generously salt the water, and then bring to a boil. Cook for 7 minutes. Strain out the water once finished. Set aside.

2. Prepare the steak by cutting it into 1-inch (2.5-cm) cubes. Place the steak bits in a bowl and season with ½ teaspoon of the pepper, ½ teaspoon of the salt, ¼ teaspoon of the garlic powder and the Worcestershire sauce. Cover and set this aside to marinate.

3. Heat a skillet (I recommend using a cast-iron one here) over medium-high heat until it gets very hot. Add 2 tablespoons (28 g) of the butter and melt. Add the potatoes and season with the remaining salt, pepper and garlic powder. Cook for 4 minutes, and then gently stir the potatoes and cook for 3 to 5 minutes, or until they're fork tender and have a golden crisp to them. Remove the potatoes from the skillet and set them aside.

4. Melt the remaining butter in the skillet and add the steak bits, rosemary and garlic. Cook the steak bits on each side for 1 minute, or until they're slightly charred and cooked to your liking. Toss the potatoes back into the skillet and stir everything together. Adjust the salt and pepper to taste. Garnish with chopped parsley.

CUMIN AVOCADO, BEAN AND CORN SALAD

This salad is a staple in my household. It's fast, easy and I usually always have the ingredients on hand! You can enjoy it on its own for a filling meal, or pair it with some grilled shrimp or chicken skewers. The flavors work so well next to my Avocado Lime Chicken Tacos (page 89) as well. This is also great as a salsa when served with chips. Win, win, win!

Yield: 4 servings

2 (15-oz [425-g]) cans corn, strained

½–1 finely diced jalapeño (depending on spice preference)

1 cup (172 g) cooked black beans

1 bunch cilantro, chopped

½ cup (40 g) diced red onion

¾ tsp cumin

½ tsp crushed red pepper flakes, or more to taste

Juice of 2 limes, or to taste

1 tsp crushed garlic

2 tbsp (30 ml) olive oil

½ tsp black pepper

Salt, to taste

2 avocados, diced

1. In a bowl, mix together the corn, jalapeño, black beans, cilantro and red onion.

2. For the dressing, add the cumin, red pepper flakes, lime juice, garlic, olive oil, pepper and salt. Mix evenly. Add the diced avocados and gently stir them in. Try not to over-mix the avocados so they hold their shape.

CHAPTER 4:
PASS *the* PASTA, PLEASE!

Pasta, I love you.

From rigatoni to linguine, farfalle to tortellini, spaghetti to fettuccine, your lines and curves amaze me. With all your various forms and perfect chew, complemented by endless options of sauces to glisten over you, your generosity is a true virtue. You specialize in brightening up somber weeknights. Lemon and Herb Farfalle (page 98) will quickly lift the mood with just a few bites. Or possibly a Spicy Pink Rigatoni (page 97) to help relax and unwind. The richness of the sauce will surely ease a troubled mind. This chapter will bring the comfort that pasta will provide. So dive in for the ultimate prize of a bowl by your side.

SPICY PINK RIGATONI

This dish has all the hype on my recipe page for a reason. Easily one of my top-three fan-favorite recipes, the decadent pink sauce is brought to life with a touch of spice and fresh basil. The garlic, tomato and basil serve up all the aromatics while the cream and butter bring on the decadence and comfort. The thick sauce perfectly coats each chewy tube of rigatoni and will have you wiping the plate clean!

Yield: 5 servings

1 lb (454 g) uncooked rigatoni pasta

2 tbsp (28 g) unsalted butter

1 tbsp (8 g) crushed garlic

2 cups (480 ml) tomato sauce

1 cup (240 ml) heavy cream

1 tsp sugar

¼ tsp black pepper

½ tsp crushed red pepper flakes, or more to taste

⅓ cup (33 g) freshly grated Parmesan cheese

½ cup (20 g) hand-torn fresh basil (see Notes)

Salt, to taste

1. Boil the pasta in salted water until it's 2 or so minutes shy of being fully cooked. Once it's ready, reserve ¼ cup (60 ml) of the pasta water, and then drain the pasta.

2. While the pasta is boiling, prepare the sauce. In a pot over medium-high heat, melt the butter and sauté the garlic until fragrant. Pour in the tomato sauce and let it simmer for 5 minutes. Add the heavy cream, sugar, black pepper and red pepper flakes. Mix and adjust the seasoning to taste. (Don't add any salt until after the pasta water and Parmesan cheese have been added so the dish isn't too salty.)

3. Lower the heat to medium-low and allow the sauce to simmer for 5 minutes, or until it has thickened. Add the pasta along with the reserved pasta water and cook over medium-high heat until the pasta is cooked al dente. Gently fold in the Parmesan and basil. Allow the parmesan to melt, and then add salt to taste. Serve while hot!

Notes: Hand-torn basil packs more flavor in dishes. The basil doesn't get bruised by the knife, and there isn't wasted basil juice and flavor that gets left behind on the cutting board!

The best way to reheat a creamy pasta is on the stovetop over medium-low heat. Add a splash of milk or cream to the pasta so that it remains creamy, and allow it to heat through.

LEMON AND HERB FARFALLE

I love anything with lemon, but pasta, butter and lemon have always been my weakness. This dish combines all that with fresh herbs, fragrant garlic and toasted pine nuts. The flavors are just incredible, and the dish is perfectly refreshing. This only takes about twenty minutes to prepare and never fails to hit the spot. Enjoy it on its own or with a protein of your choice on the side!

Yield: 3 servings

½ lb (226 g) uncooked farfalle pasta

2 tbsp (28 g) butter

2 tbsp (30 ml) olive oil, divided

2½ tsp (7 g) crushed garlic

1¼ tsp (2 g) lemon zest

¼ cup (60 ml) lemon juice

½ tsp black pepper

¼ cup (25 g) Parmesan

¼ cup (60 ml) heavy cream

Salt, to taste

⅓ cup (45 g) pine nuts

1 tbsp (3 g) packed hand-torn basil

1 tbsp (4 g) chopped tarragon

½ tbsp (2 g) sliced chives

⅓ cup (20 g) chopped parsley

1. Boil the pasta in salted water until cooked al dente.

2. Meanwhile, prepare the sauce by adding the butter and 1 tablespoon (15 ml) of the olive oil to a saucepan over medium-high heat. Once the butter melts, add the crushed garlic and cook until fragrant. Add the lemon zest, lemon juice, pepper, Parmesan and heavy cream. Season with salt to taste, and simmer for 3 to 5 minutes.

3. In a small skillet, heat the remaining olive oil over medium-high heat. Add the pine nuts and cook until they're a light, golden color, and then remove from the heat and set aside.

4. Once the pasta is cooked, strain the water out and add the pasta to the sauce. Top with the basil, tarragon, chives and parsley. Stir and cook for 2 minutes. Garnish with the toasted pine nuts and serve while hot.

CREAMY ALFREDO PENNE WITH CRISPY CHICKEN

Garlicky, creamy alfredo coats the al dente penne in this family-favorite dish. The crispy, Italian seasoned chicken is the perfect pair to go with it and provides the ultimate comfort meal. This is the classic dish we all know and love, except it's packed with extra flavor and is ultra-creamy.

Yield: 5 servings

For the Pasta

1 lb (454 g) uncooked penne pasta

For the Chicken

½ tbsp (4 g) all-purpose flour

1 tsp dried oregano, plus more for serving

1 tsp garlic powder

½ tsp black pepper

Salt, to taste

1 lb (454 g) chicken breast, sliced into thin, ¼" (6-mm) strips

1½ tbsp (23 ml) olive oil

For the Alfredo Sauce

¼ cup (57 g) butter

1 tbsp (8 g) crushed garlic

2 cups (480 ml) heavy cream

2 tbsp (29 g) cream cheese

1½ cups (150 g) freshly grated Parmesan cheese, plus more for serving

2 tsp (6 g) garlic powder

¾ tsp freshly cracked pepper

Salt, to taste

Crushed red pepper flakes (optional)

1. Cook the pasta in boiling salted water until al dente.

2. To prepare the chicken, in a large bowl, mix together the flour, oregano, garlic powder, pepper and salt. Toss the chicken in the mixture. Heat the olive oil in a deep-sided skillet and using tongs, place the chicken in. Pan fry on each side for 2 minutes, or until golden and crispy. Remove the chicken and set aside.

3. To make the sauce, melt the butter over medium-high heat in the same pot the chicken was cooked in. Add the crushed garlic and cook until fragrant. Add the heavy cream and cream cheese and let this simmer for 3 to 5 minutes, or until it's thickened. Add the Parmesan cheese, garlic powder, pepper and salt, and mix until the cheese has melted. Simmer for 2 minutes, and then add the pasta and chicken. Gently fold this together and let it simmer for 1 minute. Serve immediately and top with Parmesan, oregano and red pepper flakes (if using).

SYRIAN GARLIC YOGURT PASTA

This creamy, garlicky Pasta is a Syrian classic known as maacarona bil laban. My mother used to make a version of this almost weekly growing up, and my siblings and I would always look forward to it. This heavenly pasta is garlicky, nutty and slightly tangy. The cool yogurt sauce paired with the steaming hot meat and sizzling toasted pine nuts creates a unique dish that wins the hearts of everyone who tries it.

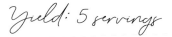

Yield: 5 servings

1 lb (454 g) uncooked pasta

3 cups (720 ml) plain yogurt

1 tbsp (8 g) crushed garlic

¼ cup (60 ml) water

Salt, to taste

1½ tbsp (23 ml) olive oil, divided

1 onion, finely diced

1 lb (454 g) ground beef

2 tsp (4 g) allspice

1 tsp black pepper

½ cup (68 g) pine nuts

½ bunch parsley, chopped

½ tsp sumac, for garnishing

½ tsp Aleppo pepper flakes, for garnishing

1. Boil the pasta in salted water until al dente.

2. While the pasta is cooking, in a large bowl, mix the yogurt, garlic, water and salt to taste. Set aside.

3. In a skillet, heat ½ tablespoon (8 ml) of the olive oil over medium-high heat. Sauté the onion until softened. Add the ground beef, allspice, pepper and salt (as desired) and break it up finely until the meat is no longer pink.

4. In a separate skillet, heat the remaining olive oil over medium-high heat and add the pine nuts. Toast for 3 to 5 minutes, stirring occasionally, until they turn a light golden color. Remove them from the heat immediately.

5. Toss the pasta with the garlic yogurt sauce, layer the beef on top, and then add the toasted pine nuts, parsley and a sprinkle of sumac and Aleppo pepper.

CAJUN SHRIMP PASTA

Cajun shrimp pasta, or this special "whole shabang pasta," is influenced by a delicious seafood boil sauce from one of my favorite restaurants. It's a mix of all the best flavors: smoky Cajun, garlic butter and lemon pepper. Enjoy this fun and dangerously delicious recipe!

Yield: 3 servings

For the Pasta

½ lb (226 g) uncooked linguine

For the Sauce

1½ tbsp (21 g) unsalted butter

1 tbsp (8 g) chopped garlic

1 cup (240 ml) heavy cream

½ tsp brown sugar

1 tsp paprika

1 tsp lemon pepper

1 tsp Old Bay Seasoning

½ tsp Cajun seasoning

½ tsp dried oregano

½ tsp garlic powder

For the Shrimp

1 tbsp (15 ml) olive oil

1 lb (454 g) jumbo shrimp, peeled and deveined, tails off

½ tsp Cajun seasoning

½ tsp garlic powder

½ tsp dried oregano

¼ tsp paprika

¼ tsp lemon pepper

¼ tsp black pepper

¼ tsp salt, or to taste

1. Boil the pasta in salted water until al dente. Reserve ¼ cup (60 ml) of the pasta water.

2. Meanwhile, prepare the sauce by heating the butter in a deep-sided skillet over medium-high heat. Add the garlic and cook until fragrant. Pour in the heavy cream and season with the brown sugar, paprika, lemon pepper, Old Bay Seasoning, Cajun seasoning, oregano and garlic powder. Simmer over medium-low heat for 10 minutes.

3. Prepare the shrimp by heating the olive oil in a separate skillet over medium-high heat. Once it's hot, add the shrimp and season with the Cajun seasoning, garlic powder, oregano, paprika, lemon pepper, pepper and salt. Toss to combine and cook on each side for 2 minutes, or until the shrimp is no longer pink.

4. Add the shrimp and the cooked and strained pasta to the sauce and gently fold them in. Pour in the reserved pasta water and simmer everything together for 2 minutes. Enjoy!

MAMA'S FAMOUS SYRIAN SPAGHETTI

Maacarona bil lahme is a simple yet delicious Middle Eastern method of making spaghetti. This dish reminds me of my beautiful mother and has me reminiscing about my childhood days. It was always a great night when my mom made this per my and my siblings' requests. Although it's just one simple ingredient, the allspice in this dish really sets this apart from your typical spaghetti. The Middle Eastern flavors come through strongly from the mixture of the tomato paste, allspice, beef and onion.

Yield: 4 servings

½ lb (226 g) uncooked spaghetti

1½ tbsp (23 ml) olive oil

½ onion, finely diced

1 lb (454 g) ground beef

½ tsp black pepper

1 tsp allspice

Salt, to taste

1 (6-oz [170-g]) can tomato paste

1 cup (240 ml) water

1 tbsp (15 ml) hot sauce (optional)

1. Cook the pasta in salted boiling water until al dente.

2. In a skillet over medium-high heat, heat the olive oil. Once hot, add the diced onion. Sauté until softened, and then add the ground beef, pepper, allspice and salt (as desired). Break the ground beef down as it cooks until it's no longer pink. Add the tomato paste and water and adjust the seasonings to taste. Add the cooked and strained spaghetti with the hot sauce (if using) and carefully mix everything together. Serve while piping hot!

CREAMY PESTO PASTA

This dish using my homemade pesto is out of this world. Because that pesto is PACKED with flavor, this pasta requires minimal work. My pasta-loving mom took one bite and yelled, "WOW!" so loud it startled me. Crowning this as the "best pasta" she's ever had is reason enough to give this one a shot! This is delicious on its own, but on occasion, I love to pair it with some shrimp or chicken.

Yield: 4 servings

For the Pesto

5 cloves garlic

2 tbsp (16 g) toasted pine nuts (see Note)

2 tbsp (16 g) regular pine nuts

1 tsp lemon zest

1 tbsp (15 ml) lemon juice

2 cups (48 g) packed basil leaves

¼ cup (25 g) freshly grated Parmesan cheese

¼ cup (26 g) freshly grated pecorino cheese

¼ tsp black pepper

½ cup (120 ml) olive oil

Salt, to taste

For the Pasta

1 lb (454 g) penne or pasta of choice

For the Sauce

2 cups (480 ml) heavy cream

¼ cup (25 g) freshly grated Parmesan cheese

¼ tsp black pepper

Salt, to taste

Crushed red pepper flakes, for garnishing

Toasted pine nuts, for garnishing

1. To make the pesto, combine the garlic, toasted pine nuts, regular pine nuts, lemon zest, lemon juice, basil, Parmesan, pecorino and pepper in a food processor. Stop and scrape the edges down a few times until all the ingredients are finely chopped. While the food processor is running, slowly drizzle in the olive oil. Season with salt to taste. Set aside.

2. Cook the pasta in salted boiling water until al dente.

3. In a deep-sided pan, prepare the sauce by adding the prepared pesto over medium-high heat. Toast the pesto until fragrant so the garlic and basil flavors have time to cook together, and then add the heavy cream. Let this come to a boil, and then lower the heat to medium-low and simmer for 5 minutes. Mix in the Parmesan cheese, pepper, salt and cooked and strained pasta and garnish with the crushed red pepper flakes and extra toasted pine nuts.

Note: For the toasted pine nuts, heat 1 teaspoon of olive oil in a small skillet. Add the 2 tablespoons (16 g) pine nuts and sauté, stirring constantly for 3 to 5 minutes over medium heat. As soon as the pine nuts turn a light golden color, remove them from the heat because they continue to cook off the heat. Don't wait for them to reach the desired color while they're still on the stovetop because they will burn once you remove them.

SHRIMP SCAMPI LINGUINE

This pasta dish is one of the quickest you can make, and this recipe will make it one of your new favorites. The ingredients are simple, but the garlic, red pepper, zesty lemon and fresh parsley bring all the best flavors to the table. The saucy, buttery noodles paired with the juicy shrimp make for the perfect weeknight meal.

Yield: 4 servings

1 lb (454 g) uncooked linguine

3 tbsp (42 g) butter, divided

3 tbsp (45 ml) olive oil, divided

1½ tbsp (12 g) crushed garlic

¼ tsp crushed red pepper flakes, or to taste

1 lb (454 g) jumbo shrimp, peeled and deveined, tails off

Salt, to taste

½ tsp black pepper, divided

⅓ cup (59 g) finely diced tomatoes (optional)

¼ cup (60 ml) lemon juice

½ tbsp (2 g) lemon zest

⅓ cup (20 g) chopped parsley

1. Boil the linguine in salted water until al dente. Reserve 1 cup (240 ml) of the pasta water before straining it out.

2. In a deep-sided pan, heat 1 tablespoon (14 g) of the butter and 1 tablespoon (15 ml) of the olive oil over medium heat. When hot, add the garlic and crushed red pepper flakes. Cook until fragrant, and then add the shrimp. Season with salt and ¼ teaspoon of the black pepper. Cook until the shrimp is no longer pink, and then remove the shrimp from the pan and onto a covered plate to keep them warm.

3. In the same pan, melt the remaining butter, and then pour in the remaining olive oil. Add the diced tomatoes (if using) and cook until slightly softened. Pour in the 1 cup (240 ml) of reserved pasta water and scrape the bottom of the pan to release all the flavors. Add the lemon juice and lemon zest and cook for 2 minutes. Season with the remaining black pepper and salt to taste. Remove the pan from the heat and add the shrimp in along with the cooked pasta and chopped parsley. Toss together and enjoy!

CHAPTER 5:
AIR FRYER *and*
INSTANT POT®
FAVORITES

The air fryer and Instant Pot have been the trendy kitchen gadgets, and I must say, I use both more than any other kitchen appliance I own. The air fryer cooks dishes much quicker than the oven, and the Instant Pot is handy with quick, one-pot dishes, making these two a home cook's best friend when it comes to quick weeknight meals. I love experimenting with recipes in these appliances and seeing the range of things that can be made in each. This chapter will provide fun, unique recipes in both the air fryer and Instant Pot that span across several different cuisines. Happy cooking!

CHICKEN AND CHEESE TAQUITOS

These crispy taquitos are simply amazing! Filled with flavor and fun, they are perfect to make for your family, friends or for yourself on a weeknight. Traditionally, this Mexican dish is filled with a flavorful beef, cheese or chicken stuffing. The crunch of the tortilla paired with the juicy, spiced filling and the saucy salsa verde and crema Mexicana on top will make your Monday feel like a Saturday night!

Yield: 3 servings

For the Chicken Filling

2½ cups (560 g) shredded cooked chicken

2 tbsp (29 g) cream cheese

1 tsp crushed garlic

¼ cup (28 g) shredded Mexican-style blend cheese

½ tsp dried oregano

½ tbsp (3 g) chili powder

1 tsp onion powder

½ tsp smoked paprika

¼ tsp black pepper

½ tsp cumin

⅓ cup (37 g) shredded Oaxaca cheese (can substitute with Monterey Jack cheese)

Salt, to taste (optional)

For the Taquitos

10 corn tortillas (approximately)

Vegetable oil, for frying

Sour cream

Guacamole

Salsa verde

Crumbled Cotija cheese

Chopped cilantro

1. To make the chicken filling, in a bowl, add the chicken, cream cheese, garlic, Mexican cheese blend, oregano, chili powder, onion powder, smoked paprika, pepper, cumin, shredded Oaxaca cheese and salt (if using) and mix well.

2. To prepare the taquitos, wrap the corn tortillas in a paper towel and microwave for 1 minute, or until soft and pliable. Add ¼ cup (56 g) of the chicken filling in a centerline across a tortilla, and then tightly roll it into a log and place the taquito seam side down. Repeat this with each of the tortillas until the chicken filling is all used up.

3. To air fry, brush each taquito with oil on all sides and air fry at 390°F (200°C) for 9 minutes, or until crispy, flipping once halfway through. For a more traditional method, you can shallow fry these instead. In a deep-sided pan over medium-high heat, heat 1 inch (2.5 cm) of vegetable oil. Once hot, add the taquitos and fry on all sides until golden and crispy. Top with sour cream, guacamole, salsa verde, Cotija and cilantro.

STICKY BBQ CORN RIBS

Last spring, I posted a recipe video for elotes-inspired corn ribs, and the video instantly went viral, hitting over 13 million views and starting a new corn ribs trend on the internet. The video was featured in many large news publications and was loved by so many. Seeing such a large reaction to the video, I just had to keep experimenting with corn ribs in the kitchen. After dabbling with a few different ideas, these sticky BBQ corn ribs were born and, oh, man, were they worth the wait. If you're a lover of anything BBQ, these will blow you away. These are way more satisfying to eat than regular corn on the cob. I love my beefy ribs, but these do not disappoint!

Yield: 3 servings

3 corncobs (makes 12 ribs)

¼ cup (60 ml) melted unsalted butter

¼ tsp chili powder

¼ tsp garlic powder

¼ tsp smoked paprika

¼ tsp black pepper

⅓ cup (80 ml) BBQ sauce of choice, warm

1. Stand the corn up straight on a cutting board. Using the sharpest knife you have, balance the center of the knife in the center of the top of the cob. Push lightly, just enough to get the knife barely stuck in the cob, and then lift the knife and corn together and bang it onto the cutting board to slice all the way through the corn. You may have to keep lifting and banging until it cuts all the way through. Take the two halves and repeat with each one, cutting the corn into four equal parts. Repeat with the remaining cobs.

2. In a bowl, mix together the melted butter, chili powder, garlic powder, smoked paprika and pepper. Generously brush this butter mixture over each of the corn wedges.

3. To cook, I air fried at 375°F (190°C) for 5 minutes on one side, and then flipped the corn ribs over and air fried for 4 minutes. Depending on the size of your air fryer, you may have to cook these in two separate batches. Be sure not to overcrowd the air fryer and that the corn ribs are arranged in an even layer. You can also bake these at 375°F (190°C) for 25 minutes, or until they've curled and slightly charred. Brush the BBQ sauce over each corn rib and serve hot.

GARLIC PARMESAN CHICKEN WINGS

These air fryer chicken wings are the crispiest wings I've ever had. They are air fried to a golden crisp and are so juicy they'll fall right off the bone. They're tossed in a garlic Parmesan butter for the most addictive weeknight meal. This needs to be a weekly treat—you deserve it!

Yield: 3 servings

For the Chicken

1½ lb (680 g) chicken wings

½ tbsp (7 g) baking powder

1 tbsp (8 g) garlic powder

1 tsp black pepper

1 tsp salt

1 tsp chili powder

1 tbsp (2 g) dried parsley

For the Garlic Parmesan Butter

¼ cup (60 ml) melted butter

1 tbsp (4 g) chopped parsley

½ tsp black pepper

4 cloves garlic, finely minced

2 tbsp (13 g) finely grated Parmesan cheese

1. To make the chicken, place the wings in a large bowl and using a paper towel, blot them dry as much as possible. The more moisture you take out, the crispier these will be! Add the baking powder for extra crisp and the garlic powder, pepper, salt, chili powder and parsley. Mix well.

2. Air fry at 380°F (190°C) for 8 minutes on each side. Turn up the heat to 400°F (200°C) and air fry for 4 minutes, or until the wings are golden and crispy. Keep in mind that different sized wings will require slightly different cook times, so keep an eye on the wings and cook for more or less time as needed.

3. While the wings are cooking, make the butter mixture by combining the melted butter, parsley, pepper, garlic and Parmesan cheese in a large bowl. Once the wings are ready, add them to the bowl with the garlic Parmesan butter and toss until the wings are fully coated.

SWEET AND SMOKY DRUMSTICKS

These drumsticks are an exciting weeknight meal that will have you licking your fingers clean. The marinade is so delicious and tastes like the chicken has been slow cooked in a smoker. For something so quick and easy, these really tick every box for the perfect meal. I recommend pairing these with some roasted veggies and steamed rice!

Yield: 2 servings

¼ cup (60 ml) honey

2 tsp (3 g) paprika

2 tsp (3 g) smoked paprika

2 tbsp (10 g) Cajun seasoning

2 tsp (3 g) chili powder

2 tsp (6 g) garlic powder

1 tsp black pepper

1 tsp salt, or to taste

3½ tbsp (53 ml) avocado or vegetable oil

6 chicken drumsticks

1. Heat up the honey in the microwave for 20 seconds. In a large bowl, mix the honey, paprika, smoked paprika, Cajun seasoning, chili powder, garlic powder, pepper, salt and oil until a smooth red paste is formed. Add the drumsticks and score the chicken all over so the marinade flavors the chicken to the bone.

2. Spray the air fryer with nonstick cooking spray, and then place the drumsticks inside. Air fry at 380°F (190°C) for 8 minutes, and then flip and cook for 12 to 15 minutes, flipping every 5 minutes. Depending on the size of your drumsticks and the air fryer being used (I've noticed different air fryers cook slightly differently) you may have to keep an eye on the drumsticks towards the end. Cook until the internal temperature has reached 165°F (75°C).

HERB AND PEPPER POTATOES

If you've been following my social media pages for a while, you know I love me a good potato recipe. These herb and pepper potatoes bring everything to the table: a crispy exterior with a nice snap; a soft and fluffy interior; and intense garlic, herb and pepper flavors. These are such a comforting weeknight treat and are so fast to make. You can enjoy these on their own as I often do, but these + steak = pure bliss.

Yield: 3 servings

¼ cup (60 ml) olive oil

½ tbsp (1 g) finely chopped rosemary

½ tbsp (1 g) fresh thyme

1 tbsp (3 g) finely chopped basil

1 tbsp (4 g) finely chopped parsley

1 tsp garlic powder

½ tsp black pepper

½ tsp crushed red pepper flakes

Salt, to taste

1½ lb (680 g) fingerling potatoes, sliced in half lengthwise

¼ cup (60 ml) sour cream

¼ cup (60 ml) plain yogurt

½ tbsp (4 g) crushed garlic

1. In a bowl, combine the olive oil, rosemary, thyme, basil, parsley, garlic powder, pepper, red pepper flakes and salt. Mix and adjust the salt to taste, and then add in the potatoes and toss until they're fully coated.

2. Air fry at 400°F (200°C) for 10 minutes, and then shake the basket and air fry for 5 minutes, or until golden and crispy on the outside and soft and fluffy on the inside.

3. While the potatoes are cooking, prepare the dipping sauce. In a bowl mix the sour cream, plain yogurt, crushed garlic and salt to taste. Serve next to the potatoes and enjoy!

MASALA CHICKEN BURGERS

These masala chicken patties take burgers to a whole new level. Ditch the grill and use the air fryer for these super juicy and flavorful burgers. The delicious spice blend, garlic, onion, ginger, pepper and cilantro flavor these patties to perfection. This also makes for a perfect kebab mixture if you'd like to form them into kebabs instead and serve with some basmati rice. You can get so creative with this recipe, so have fun!

Yield: 4 servings

1 lb (454 g) ground chicken

1 jalapeño, deseeded and finely diced

1 tbsp (8 g) crushed garlic

½ tbsp (4 g) grated ginger

⅓ cup (53 g) finely diced red onions

¼ cup (4 g) finely chopped cilantro

½ tsp black pepper

1 tsp chili powder

1 tsp paprika

½ tbsp (4 g) garam masala

½ tsp cumin

¾ tsp turmeric

¼ tsp ground cardamom

½ tbsp (9 g) salt, or to taste

1 tbsp (15 ml) olive oil

For Serving

4 burger buns

Sliced red onion

Sliced tomato

Lettuce

1. In a large bowl, combine the chicken, jalapeño, garlic, ginger, red onions, cilantro, pepper, chili powder, paprika, garam masala, cumin, turmeric, cardamom, salt and olive oil. Mix until well combined.

2. Slightly wet your hands, and then form the mixture into four patties that are ½ inch (1.3 cm) thick. Lightly grease the air fryer tray and cook the patties for 15 minutes at 370°F (190°C), flipping once halfway through, or until the internal temperature reaches 165°F (75°C). Be sure not to overcrowd the air fryer (you may need to do two batches).

3. Place the patties in burger buns with sliced red onion, tomato, lettuce and your other favorite burger toppings and spreads!

ZESTY MEDITERRANEAN POTATO SALAD

This super zesty potato salad is made so quickly using the Instant Pot. The potatoes soak up the fresh herbs, garlic, lemon and spices so beautifully. I still remember the first time I tasted this dish when my mother made it for dinner one night. The fresh and tangy flavors with the fluffy potatoes won my heart instantly. I'm a sucker for a good potato dish, and this one is sure to satisfy you and your family.

Yield: 5 servings

4 russet potatoes, peeled and diced into 1" (2.5-cm) cubes

2 tsp (6 g) crushed garlic

3 scallions, thinly sliced

¼ cup (23 g) finely chopped fresh mint

½ bunch parsley, finely chopped

1 tsp Aleppo pepper flakes or crushed red pepper flakes

¼ tsp black pepper

½ tsp allspice

½ tsp cumin

¼ cup + 2 tbsp (90 ml) lemon juice

¼ cup (60 ml) olive oil

Salt, to taste

1. Fill the Instant Pot with enough salted water to cover the diced potatoes. Be sure to heavily salt the water so the insides of the potatoes aren't bland.

2. Set the Instant Pot to pressure cook on high for 3 minutes. Make sure the top valve is set to sealing. Once the time is up, turn the valve to venting for a quick release. Once they're ready, strain the potatoes and set aside to cool.

3. While the potatoes are cooking, in a large bowl, mix together the garlic, scallions, mint, parsley, Aleppo pepper, pepper, allspice, cumin, lemon juice, olive oil and salt. Add the cooked potatoes and mix until fully coated, and then serve.

GARLIC LEMON CHICKEN AND POTATOES

Garlic and lemon lovers, rejoice! This dish is more commonly known as jaj w batata. It's a classic Middle Eastern dish that is so perfect for an easy and delicious dinner. I used to get so excited as a child when my mother made this. It combines all my favorite flavors: juicy, succulent chicken; soft, pillowy potatoes; and a divine sauce made of garlic, lemon juice, olive oil and the perfect subtle kick of black pepper.

Yield: 3 servings

3 tbsp (45 ml) olive oil

1 lb (454 g) chicken breast, cut into 1" (2.5-cm) cubes

1 lb (454 g) baby yellow potatoes, halved (or peeled russet potatoes cut into 1" [2.5-cm] cubes)

1 tbsp (18 g) salt, or as desired

2½ tsp (5 g) black pepper

1 tsp allspice

½ tsp turmeric

½ cup (120 ml) lemon juice

1½ tbsp (12 g) crushed garlic

1 cup (240 ml) chicken broth

Chopped parsley, for serving

Pita bread, for serving

1. Set the Instant Pot to the sauté setting. Pour in the olive oil and once hot, add the chicken breast cubes. Sauté for 1 minute, and then add the potatoes, salt, pepper, allspice, turmeric, lemon juice, garlic and chicken broth.

2. Set the Instant Pot to pressure cook on high for 7 minutes. Make sure the top valve is set to sealing. Once the time is up, turn the valve to venting for a quick release. Top with chopped parsley, and serve with warm pita bread to scoop it all up!

CAJUN SHRIMP AND POTATO BOIL

These juicy shrimp, fluffy potatoes and sweet corn are cooked in a buttery, garlic, Cajun and lemon pepper sauce. While you're eating this, you won't believe it came together so quickly. It's delicious, the flavors are complex and it's such a complete meal that takes minimal prep and cook time. This is a great meal to enjoy with some family or friends because it's so easy to double the recipe!

Yield: 5 servings

¼ cup (57 g) unsalted butter

1 lb (454 g) baby potatoes, halved

¼ cup (32 g) minced garlic

3 corncobs, cut widthwise into 3 pieces each

3 cups (720 ml) chicken broth

2 tbsp (30 ml) lemon juice

1 tsp smoked paprika

1 tsp brown sugar

½ tbsp (3 g) salt

½ tsp ginger powder

½ tsp Old Bay seasoning

2 lb (907 g) extra jumbo shrimp, peeled and deveined

Lime wedges, for serving

Chopped parsley, for serving

1. Set the Instant Pot to sauté and add the butter. Once melted, add the potatoes, garlic, corn, chicken broth, lemon juice, smoked paprika, brown sugar, salt, ginger powder and Old Bay seasoning. Stir and then cover with the lid and set to pressure cook on high for 4 minutes. Once the time is up, turn the valve to venting for a quick release.

2. Once it has fully vented, open the lid and set the Instant Pot back to the sauté setting. Add the shrimp and cook for 5 minutes, or until the shrimp is pink and cooked through. Serve with lime wedges and garnish with chopped parsley.

BEST EVER SLOPPY JOES

These Instant Pot sloppy joes live up to their name, and I love every bit of them. The sloppier the joe, the better it tastes. Saucy, sweet, smoky, peppery . . . the flavors in this are out of this world. The toasted bun perfectly soaks up that incredible juicy and saucy beef. They're quick to whip up and will definitely satisfy your taste buds!

Yield: 5 servings

1 tbsp (15 ml) olive oil

½ tbsp (4 g) crushed garlic

1 onion, finely diced, plus more for serving

1 bell pepper, finely diced

1 lb (454 g) ground beef

1 tsp garlic powder

½ tsp black pepper

1 tsp chili powder

1 tsp onion powder

1 tsp salt

½ tsp cayenne

½ tsp smoked paprika

2 tbsp (32 g) tomato paste

¾ cup (180 ml) ketchup

2½ tbsp (35 g) brown sugar

2 tbsp (30 ml) Worcestershire sauce

1 tbsp (15 ml) mustard

1 tbsp (15 ml) vinegar

½ tsp liquid smoke

½ tbsp (8 ml) soy sauce

⅓ cup (80 ml) beef broth

1 tbsp (8 g) cornstarch

¼ cup (60 ml) water

5 brioche buns, for serving

Sliced pickles, for serving

1. Set the Instant Pot to sauté and add the olive oil. Once hot, add the garlic, onion and bell pepper. Sauté for 2 minutes, or until tender. Add the ground beef and immediately begin to break it up finely. Season with the garlic powder, pepper, chili powder, onion powder, salt, cayenne and smoked paprika. Mix it all in as you continue to break up the meat.

2. Once the meat is no longer pink, add the tomato paste, ketchup, brown sugar, Worcestershire sauce, mustard, vinegar, liquid smoke, soy sauce and beef broth. Stir everything together, and then pressure cook on high for 5 minutes.

3. In a bowl, stir the cornstarch and water together until fully combined. Once the cook time is done, turn the valve to venting for a quick release. Then, open the lid and stir in the cornstarch slurry. Set the Instant Pot to sauté and cook for 5 minutes so that the cornstarch slurry has time to thicken.

4. Toast the buns in a pan over medium-high heat, and then fill each bun with a generous amount of the cooked meat. Serve with your choice of diced onions and sliced pickles.

AROMATIC BUTTER CHICKEN

This recipe is always a huge hit, and my Instant Pot version is a lifesaver when you need a quick weeknight pick-me-up. I've always been a huge sucker for a good butter chicken, and this homemade one truly brings on the flavor. The sauce is creamy and well spiced, and the chicken is juicy and tender. Try it with some garlic naan and/or basmati rice.

Yield: 4 servings

1 tbsp (15 ml) olive oil
1 onion, finely diced
1 jalapeño, finely diced
1 tbsp (8 g) crushed garlic
1 tsp minced ginger
2½ tbsp (40 g) tomato paste
1½ lb (680 g) chicken thighs, cut into 1" (2.5-cm) cubes
1 cup (240 ml) tomato sauce
2 tbsp (30 ml) lemon juice
¾ cup (180 ml) chicken broth
2 tsp (4 g) cumin
½ tbsp (3 g) paprika
1 tsp turmeric
1 tbsp (6 g) garam masala
½ tsp cayenne
1 tsp onion powder
1 tsp chili powder
1 tsp dried coriander
¼ tsp cardamom
¼ tsp cinnamon
2 tsp (10 g) sugar
Salt, as desired
1 cup (240 ml) heavy cream
2½ tbsp (35 g) butter
Chopped cilantro, for garnishing

1. Set the Instant Pot to sauté, and add the olive oil. Once the oil is hot, add the onion, jalapeño, garlic and ginger. Cook for 2 minutes, or until fragrant. Add the tomato paste and chicken and sauté for 2 minutes. Add the tomato sauce, lemon juice, chicken broth, cumin, paprika, turmeric, garam masala, cayenne, onion powder, chili powder, coriander, cardamom, cinnamon, sugar and salt. Stir the sauce and chicken and then lock on the lid and pressure cook on high for 7 minutes.

2. Once the timer is up, turn the valve to venting for a quick release. Then, remove the lid and stir in the heavy cream and butter. Garnish with chopped cilantro.

SPICED NICE CHILI

This chili recipe is so special to me and has been winning the hearts of my lovely followers left and right for the past three years. I've now been tweaking this recipe for eleven years, and it is one of my favorite dishes to make. This chili packs on the flavor heavy and wows everyone from the very first bite. The scent will make your house feel like a home and is the perfect meal for a weeknight. Make this for yourself and your loved ones for a cozy and delicious meal!

Yield: 5 servings

½ tbsp (8 ml) olive oil

1 onion, finely diced

3 cloves garlic, minced

½ jalapeño, finely diced

½ (6-oz [170-g]) can tomato paste

1 lb (454 g) ground beef (you can also use ground chicken or turkey)

2 tbsp + ½ tsp (15 g) chili powder

2½ tsp (5 g) cumin

1 tbsp (7 g) paprika

1 tsp smoked paprika

½ tbsp (4 g) garlic powder

½ tbsp (4 g) onion powder

½ tsp cayenne (adjust to your preferred spice level)

1¼ tsp (3 g) black pepper

1¼ tsp (6 g) sugar

2½ tsp (4 g) dried oregano

½ tbsp (3 g) allspice

¼ tsp nutmeg

½ large juicy diced tomato or ½ (15-oz [425-g]) can diced tomatoes

½ (15-oz [425-g]) can crushed tomatoes

½ (15-oz [425-g]) can tomato sauce

2 cups (480 ml) low-sodium chicken broth or water

1 (15-oz [425-g]) can kidney beans

½ (15-oz [425-g]) can black beans

½ (15-oz [425-g]) can pinto beans

Salt, to taste

For Serving (optional)

Shredded cheese

Avocado

Sour cream

Sliced scallions

Lime wedges

Sliced jalapeño

1. Set the Instant Pot to sauté. Add the olive oil, and once it gets hot, add the onion, garlic and jalapeño. Cook for 2 minutes, or until slightly softened. Add the tomato paste and cook for about 2 minutes, or until it deepens in color. Add the ground beef and break it down very finely. Add the chili powder, cumin, paprika, smoked paprika, garlic powder, onion powder, cayenne, pepper, sugar, oregano, allspice and nutmeg. Mix while continuing to break up and cook the meat until it is cooked through and no longer pink. Stir in the diced tomatoes, crushed tomatoes, tomato sauce, chicken broth, kidney beans, black beans, pinto beans and salt.

2. Lock the lid on. Set the time to 15 minutes on the chili/bean cook setting, and then allow the Instant Pot to naturally release. Mix well before serving! Top with shredded cheese, avocado, sour cream, scallions, lime wedges and/or jalapeño.

ACKNOWLEDGMENTS

This book is possible because of the wonderful support system I'm blessed to have in my life, along with the wonderful team at Page Street Publishing.

A massive special thank-you to Marissa Giambelluca of Page Street Publishing for providing me with this opportunity and believing in me and my recipes. After speaking to different publishers, I knew after only one phone call that I wanted to work with you. Your kind, open-minded approach was comforting, to say the least. Thank you for being patient with me and making it a priority for this book to be something I am proud of. Your concern with me being able to keep my voice throughout the publication of this book has put me at so much ease and is so greatly appreciated. A special thank-you to Meg Palmer of the Page Street Publishing team for being a guide through any questions or troubles throughout the process. Your prompt responses and kind tone were such a comfort.

Thank you, endlessly, to my beloved mother, Abir, and father, Ziad. Everything I do is to make you proud, and I hope that is what you feel when you hold this book in your hands. Because of the safe and loving childhood you provided me with, I have the passion for cooking that flourished at a young age. Because of your constant hard work to make a happy and comfortable life for us, I learned how to be dedicated and ambitious enough to get me to this point in my career. Because of the love and reassurance you always provided me, I was able to believe in myself and pursue my dreams. Thank you for merely existing. I love you both with all my heart.

This book could not have been possible without my lovely husband, Tarek. This entire phase in my life started because of your support and encouragement to begin my Instagram food page. For the past three years, you have motivated me to be the best in my food photography, video editing and social media development. You believed in me endlessly and constantly pushed me to break out of my comfort zone, which is what has made an opportunity like this possible. Thank you for constantly telling me, randomly throughout the day, that you are proud of me. It always inspires me to work harder so I can continue to make you proud. Thank you for holding my hand and comforting me through some of the struggles and anxiety that come with putting yourself and your passion out there on social media. Your comfort has done everything for my mental health.

Thank you to my amazing family: my brothers, Tarik and Taha, and sisters, Raghad, Layla, Hanna, Ayah and Rama. Tarik, thank you for being my number-one garlic sauce hype man and maybe, not so secretly, my favorite. Thank you for supporting me in everything I do, and for always being there for me. Thank you, Taha, the absolute best brother-in-law, who has massively supported me in all my endeavors. Your encouragement and words of support have meant so much to me. Raghad, thank you for being an inspiration with your delicious SavvyChef blog. It was always so inspiring watching the creative meals you would whip up. Layla, some of my earliest memories are helping you in the kitchen while you'd bake up a storm. Thank you for including me in those moments when all I likely did was make a mess for you or nibble at everything in my sight. Hanna, thank you for inspiring me to perfect every single recipe, because if something was ever slightly off, I could count on you to point it out. Kidding! Thank you for being there for me to always vent to. Thank you for the support you've always had for Spiced Nice and for being a shoulder I could always lean on. Ayah, thank you for being so supportive throughout my entire journey as a food blogger. You are always the first one to comment and show your support, and I have always appreciated it so much.

You're a kind soul and I'm lucky to call you my sister. Rama, thank you for constantly showing your support and making me feel like I can accomplish anything. Becoming your sister in itself was the biggest gift, and you constantly inspire me by pursuing your own dreams as well. Thank you to my niece, Amar, and my nephews, Zane and Ameen, for being the biggest fans of my food. I love you all!

A heartfelt thank you to Sawsan and Chaker Mustapha, my dearest mother and father-in-law, for treating me with nothing but kindness and love. I appreciate and love you both more than I could express. Thank you for pushing me to aim high in all my career goals and for believing in me. You are both a massive inspiration to me. An even bigger thank-you for raising the best human I know. Tarek is my rock through everything.

Thank you to my sister friends who are my constant and daily support systems: Dania Mohammad, Nesma Nuru, Sara Diab, Masah Ascha, Zunera Bukhari and Nora Mohammad. Thank you for putting up with my venting and for endlessly supporting me in everything I do. You are all nothing less than family to me.

Dania, thank you for always going above and beyond for me. Thank you for doing everything you can to help, support, listen to, and most importantly, be there for me. You always show up to help, even when I have insisted that you don't, whether it be in the middle of the night or a workday for you. I cannot believe how much you've done for me, and I will always be grateful for you. Your presence in my life is the biggest blessing!

Nesma, thank you for being my biggest hype woman. You were the first Spiced Nice recipe tester! You have always encouraged me to accomplish big things. Your words of comfort and constant willingness to help have meant so much to me throughout this entire process.

Your support and energy throughout each milestone in my career have touched my heart. The way you believe in me has helped me believe in myself. You are always my source of comfort and my favorite shoulder to cry on. I am so grateful to have someone so kind, thoughtful, and supportive in my life.

Susu, Masah and Zoni, you are my sisters, and your support in everything I do means the world to me. You were the first to see my passion for cooking grow at all our hangouts and sleepovers. I love you all and am lucky to have grown up with such loving and supportive best friends by my side.

Nora, thank you for all your constant support and HELP. You never sit down as long as I'm still standing in the kitchen. You have been a massive help to me and are one of the few people I find comfort in having in the kitchen with me. And you know how rare that is for me. I love you!

Last but not least, thank you to my loyal and kind Spiced Nice followers. You are all a family to me, and the support you've given me and my recipes has encouraged me to further pursue this dream of mine. I hope to continue making you all proud and to continue satisfying your taste buds. Thank you for believing in me and the recipes I put out. Thank you for engaging with my content and making me feel seen. Thank you for your kind messages of support that bring tears to my eyes. I love you and am thankful for you all more than I could ever express. Each and every one of you has made this possible for me, and you have all touched my heart in your own unique ways.

ABOUT THE AUTHOR

Farrah Jalanbo is a first-generation Syrian American who was born and raised in Southern California. She is the woman behind the popular Instagram recipe page @spiced.nice and the TikTok page @spicednice. She first launched her Instagram recipe page three years ago and has gained a loyal following since. Her passion for cooking started at age seven and was inspired by her talented mother. Farrah has a degree in English literature from the University of Berkeley, California. Her ideal night out consists of trying new cuisines and local hole-in-the-wall spots, as well as tackling the scariest escape rooms. Farrah has been featured in many media publications, including Tasty.co, *Harper's Bazaar*, BuzzFeed Food, Yahoo News, *Today* and many more.

INDEX